TALK
THAT
TALK

How the Right Words Turn
Negative Thoughts into Positive Vibes

Robert Lawson Jr.

1st edition, October 2023
ISBN-13: 979-8-218-28037-6
Printed in the United States of America

Table of Contents

Table of Contents with Descriptors

Family & Love

Dive into the heart of relationships, where bonds are forged and love is the anchor. Whether navigating familial ties, seeking deeper connections, or yearning for romantic love, this section offers affirmations to strengthen, heal, and celebrate the ties that bind. If your heart seeks solace or joy in the realm of relationships, start here.

Health & Well-being

Your body and mind are the temples of your spirit. If you're facing health challenges, seeking mental peace, or aiming for physical and emotional balance, this section offers affirmations to rejuvenate, heal, and inspire. For a holistic approach to well-being, this is your sanctuary.

Mindfulness & Focus

Find your center in a world buzzing with distractions. If you're struggling with concentration, seeking inner peace, or aiming to be more present in the moment, these affirmations guide you towards clarity and mindfulness. For those seeking to anchor themselves in the now, this section beckons.

Professional Success

Climb the ladder of your aspirations with confidence. Whether at a career crossroads, aiming for a promotion, or starting a new venture, these affirmations fuel your professional journey. If success, ambition, and growth are on your mind, let this section be your guide.

Purpose & Direction

Navigate life's maze with a clear sense of purpose. If you're questioning your path, seeking your true calling, or wanting to align more with your life's mission, these affirmations light the way. For souls seeking their true north, this section is your compass.

Resilience & Determination

Life's storms are no match for a resilient spirit. If you're facing challenges, feeling defeated, or need a boost of determination, these affirmations will fortify your spirit. This section stands tall for those needing to harness inner strength and grit.

Self-Esteem & Confidence

Stand tall in the mirror of self-worth. If doubts cloud your reflection, if you seek to embrace your true self with more love and confidence, these affirmations are your affirming echo. For a boost of self-love and empowerment, delve into this section.

Self-Improvement & Growth

The journey of a lifetime begins with a single step towards self-improvement. If you're on a quest for personal growth, seeking to learn, or wanting to evolve, these affirmations nurture your aspirations. For souls on a transformative journey, this section is your roadmap.

Service & Philanthropy

Enrich the world with the wealth of kindness. If you're looking to give back, seeking purpose in service, or aiming to make a difference, these affirmations inspire altruistic endeavors. For hearts seeking to serve and uplift, this section is your beacon.

Social Confidence

Navigate the dance of social interactions with grace. If you're looking to overcome shyness, enhance your social skills, or feel more at ease in groups, these affirmations are your guiding star. This section lights the way for those aiming to shine in social settings.

Spiritual Connection

Embark on a soulful journey towards the divine. If you seek a deeper spiritual connection, yearning for inner peace, or want to strengthen your faith, these affirmations resonate with spiritual truths. This section is your sanctuary for souls craving for divine connection and enlightenment.

Preface: The Power of Affirmation in Every Walk of Life

Hello, dear reader! Welcome to "*Talk That Talk: How the Right Words Turn Negative Thoughts into Positive Vibes*." If you've picked up this book, it's no accident. Whether you're a student grappling with the pressures of academia, a corporate executive navigating the complexities of leadership, a mother balancing work and family, an entrepreneur facing the uncertainties of a startup, or an artist seeking inspiration, this book is crafted just for you. It's a testament to anyone and everyone who believes in the transformative power of words and the magic they can weave in our lives.

Life, as we know it, is a journey—a journey filled with peaks of joy and valleys of challenges. Sometimes, the road ahead is smooth, sunlit, and inviting. At other times, it's riddled with potholes, shadows, and unexpected turns. But here's the thing: our mindset, our beliefs, and the words we tell ourselves can make all the difference. They can be the beacon that guides us through the darkest nights or the anchor that keeps us grounded during life's storms. Let's keep winning, no matter the terrain, no matter the weather.

Now, you might wonder, why a book on affirmations? Why now? We live in a world that's constantly buzzing. A world where we're often drowned in a sea of external voices - from social media, news, peers, and sometimes, even our inner critic. Amidst all this noise, it's easy to lose our voice, sense of self, and direction. That's where this book steps in. It's not just a collection of affirmations; it's a compass, a guide, a friend. It's a reminder that amidst the chaos, a voice within you is waiting to be heard and guide you.

This book is also a tribute to the timeless wisdom of the ages, rooted deeply in biblical principles. The Bible, in its essence, is a treasure trove of affirmations. Stories of faith, hope, love, and miracles. Stories that remind us of the power of words, of belief, of staying true to our purpose. When God said, "*Let there be light*," light appeared. When Jesus said to the storm, "*Peace, be still*," the winds and waves obeyed. These aren't just stories; they're affirmations of faith, of the power of words spoken with conviction.

So, as you flip through these pages, I invite you to embark on a journey—a journey of self-discovery, of faith, of transformation. Dive deep into each section, resonate with the stories, reflect on the affirmations, and most importantly, find your voice. This book is a mirror, reflecting the immense potential, the divine spark within you. It's a call to action, a nudge to rise, shine, and embrace your true self.

Remember, dear reader, life is not about the destination; it's about the journey. And on this journey, with the right words, the right mindset, and a heart full of faith, there's no challenge too big, no mountain too high. You got this. Let's keep winning, one affirmation at a time. And as you embark on this transformative journey, remember that you're not alone. I'm with you, cheering you on, believing in you. Let's do this together. Let's talk that talk.

And as always, God bless.

How to Read/Use This Book

Welcome to a unique reading experience! "*Talk that Talk: How the Right Words Turn Negative Thoughts into Positive Vibes*" isn't your standard cover-to-cover narrative. Instead, it's a spiritual toolkit, a reservoir of strength, and a guide to navigating the myriad challenges of life. Here's a deeper dive into how you can harness the power of this book:

1. Identify Your Need

Before diving in, take a moment. Breathe. Reflect on your current state of mind. Are you grappling with self-doubt? Is there a relationship that's causing heartache? Or perhaps you're at a crossroads in your career? Pinpointing your emotional or spiritual needs is the first step. Remember, this book is designed to cater to diverse aspects of life. It's like a buffet; you pick what resonates with your current situation.

2. Navigate with Purpose

The table of contents isn't just a list; it's your roadmap. Each section is meticulously crafted to address specific challenges or emotions. So, if you're feeling a lack of direction in your professional life, the "Professional Success" section is your go-to. If it's a matter of the heart, "Family & Love" awaits. The beauty of this book is its flexibility. It's here to serve your needs, whatever they might be.

3. Deep Dive into the Chosen Section

Once you've identified the relevant section, immerse yourself. Start with the introductory story. These tales, rooted in biblical principles and set against the backdrop of the 21st century, offer solace and guidance. They're not just stories; they're mirrors reflecting common human experiences. See yourself in them and learn from them.

4. Combat Negativity with Affirmations

After the story, you'll encounter examples of negative self-talk. These are the whispers of doubt, the chains that often bind us. Recognize, confront, and then combat them with the positive affirmations that follow. These affirmations are your weapons, your shields against the arrows of negativity. They're not just words; they're mantras. Repeat them, believe in them, live them.

5. Engage with Reflection

The reflection questions are there for a reason. They're prompts to introspect, to delve deep into your psyche. Grab a pen, use the blank pages provided, and jot down your thoughts. There's power in penning down feelings. It's therapeutic and cathartic. It's a way to confront and, eventually, conquer.

6. Make It a Habit

This book isn't meant for a one-time read. It's a lifelong companion. Life will throw curveballs, challenges will arise, and emotions will ebb and flow. In those moments, come back to this book. Maybe it's "Self-Esteem & Confidence" that resonates today, but a month down the line, it could be "Mindfulness & Focus." Let the book grow with you, guide you, and be your beacon.

7. Share & Discuss

Words have more power when shared. Discuss them with friends, family, or fellow readers. Start a book club, create a discussion group, or simply share a quote on social media. When insights are shared, they multiply. They transform from mere words to movements.

8. Celebrate Small Wins

Every affirmation you resonate with, every negative thought you combat, every reflection that leads to a positive action is a win. Celebrate it. Remember, life isn't about grand victories; it's about these small, significant wins that pave the path to a larger triumph.

In essence, this book is more than just pages filled with words. It's a journey, a guide, a friend, and a mentor. It's here to remind you that, no matter the challenge, *"You got this."* Dive in with an open heart, and let's keep winning. God bless.

The Biblical Power of Positive Self-Talk

Words, in their essence, are more than mere sounds or symbols on a page. They are carriers of energy, intent, and power. The Bible, a reservoir of divine wisdom, has always emphasized the unparalleled power of words. It's a theme that resonates from Genesis to Revelation. But before we delve into the scriptures, let me share a personal chapter from my life.

At the age of 20, I experienced a profound transformation. It wasn't brought about by a self-help book, a motivational seminar, or even a life-altering event. It was a spiritual awakening, a moment of surrender and acceptance, when I gave my life to Christ. Before this pivotal moment, I tried to be a good person, to lead a life of integrity and purpose. But despite my best efforts, something always felt amiss. There was a void, an emptiness that no worldly pursuit could fill.

It was only when I began to immerse myself in the teachings of the Bible, applying its timeless principles to my daily life, that I truly began to flourish. The void was filled with a divine presence, guiding, comforting, and empowering me in ways I had never imagined. This book, "*Talk That Talk*," and the person I am today, are testaments to the transformative power of God's word and the principles it upholds.

Let's journey back to the beginning. In Genesis, the very act of creation was initiated by words: *"And God said, 'Let there be light,' and there was light."* This wasn't just a poetic expression; it was a demonstration of the sheer potency of words spoken with intent and belief. When aligned with faith and positive intent, our words have the power to shape our reality and manifest our desires, hopes, and dreams.

Consider the story of David and Goliath. A young shepherd boy, armed with nothing but a sling and a few stones, faced a giant warrior. To the onlookers, David was hopelessly outmatched. But David had something more potent than physical weapons; he had unwavering faith and the words to affirm it. He declared, *"The Lord who delivered me from the paw of the lion and from the paw of the bear will deliver me from the hand of this Philistine."* And he triumphed. His words of faith, combined with his actions, defied the odds.

Proverbs 18:21 succinctly captures this essence: *"Death and life are in the power of the tongue."* Our words can build or break, heal or harm, uplift or pull down. Every affirmation in this book, every positive declaration, is rooted in this biblical principle. When we affirm, *"I am divinely guided in every step I take,"* we're not just practicing positive self-talk; we're aligning ourselves with a higher power, tapping into a divine energy that propels us forward.

In Mark 11:23, Jesus said, *"Whoever says to this mountain, 'Be taken up and thrown into the sea,' and does not doubt in his heart, but believes that what he says will come to pass, it will be done for him."* This isn't just about moving physical mountains. It's about the challenges, the obstacles, the 'mountains' we face in our lives. With faith and the right words, we can overcome, we can triumph, and we can manifest our heart's desires.

My journey with Christ has taught me that our self-belief, combined with positive affirmations, aligns seamlessly with faith, painting vibrant pictures on life's canvas. It's a dance of the divine and the human, a synergy of faith and action. This book is an invitation to join this dance, to harness the power of positive self-talk rooted in biblical wisdom.

I share this with you not as a preacher from a pulpit but as a friend who has walked the path, faced the storms, and found solace in the divine embrace. Let's keep winning, let's keep affirming, and let's keep faith at the forefront. Because with God, all things are possible. God bless.

Share the Blessings

In life's intricate tapestry, every thread, every story, and every victory matters. Your journey, with its highs and lows, its moments of doubt, and bursts of revelation, is a testament to the enduring human spirit. And if this book has played even a small role in guiding, uplifting, or transforming your path, then it's a shared victory. A victory not just for you, but for every soul out there seeking direction, hope, and affirmation.

But here's the beautiful part: blessings, when shared, multiply. They ripple out, touching lives in ways we might never even fathom. So, if you've found solace, strength, or inspiration in these pages, I urge you to pass it on. Gift this book to a friend navigating a storm, a colleague facing a crossroad, or a loved one in need of a beacon. Your gesture might just be the lifeline they've been seeking.

Moreover, your feedback, your stories, and your experiences breathe life into this endeavor. Please leave a review, share your journey, or reach out to me directly. Every word you share becomes a beacon for someone else, guiding them through their darkest nights and into the dawn of new possibilities.

In this vast universe, our connections, our shared stories, and our collective victories are the threads that weave us together. By sharing, you're not just passing on a book; you're passing on hope, faith, and the promise of a brighter tomorrow. Let's keep winning together, and as always, God bless.

Family & Love

"Family is not an important thing, it's everything."
- Michael J. Fox

"The love of a family is life's greatest blessing."
- Eva Burrows

"In family life, love is the oil that eases friction."
- Friedrich Nietzsche

"The memories we make with our family is everything."
- Candace Cameron Bure

"Love begins at home, and it is not how much we do, but how much love we put in the action that we do."
- Mother Teresa

The Garden of Hearts: Nurturing Bonds in a Modern World

In a world dominated by technology, where connections are often measured by the number of followers or likes, the essence of true family and love can sometimes feel lost. But just like a garden, relationships require nurturing, patience, and understanding. Drawing from biblical principles, we're reminded that the foundation of all relationships is love, and love is patient, kind, and forgiving.

In a bustling city, where everyone was always in a hurry, lived Anna, a young woman trying to balance her demanding job, her family, and her love life. One day, feeling overwhelmed, she visited her grandmother, who lived on the outskirts, tending to a beautiful garden.

Anna expressed her frustrations, especially about her strained relationship with her brother and the challenges in her romantic relationship. While pruning a rose bush, her grandmother began to share the biblical story of the Prodigal Son. It was a tale of mistakes, redemption, and a father's unwavering love. She explained, "*Just like this rose bush, relationships have thorns, challenges. But with care, patience, and love, they bloom beautifully.*"

Inspired, Anna began her journey of mending her relationships, armed with affirmations:

"I am patient and understanding, allowing love to guide my actions."

"Every challenge in my relationship is an opportunity for growth."

"I deserve love and give love freely."

"Forgiveness is my strength; it heals and renews."

"Let's keep winning, for love conquers all."

Anna took her grandmother's advice to heart. She began setting aside 'unplugged' hours dedicated solely to her family and loved ones. She practiced active listening, ensuring she was present in every conversation. *"Remember,"* her grandmother had said, *"love isn't just a feeling; it's an action. Show it, express it, live it. You got this."*

Months later, Anna's relationships flourished. The bond with her brother was stronger than ever, and she found depth and understanding in her romantic relationship. She often found herself reflecting on her journey, understanding that relationships, like gardens, require time, attention, and love. As she did, she felt a profound connection with the biblical teachings, realizing that timeless wisdom was relevant even in today's digital age.

Examples of Negative Self-Talk for "Family & Love"

"They probably don't care about me."

"I'm always the one making an effort."

"Maybe I'm just unlovable."

"I don't think we can ever get past this."

"I'm not good enough for them."

"They'd be better off without me."

"I always ruin relationships."

"No one understands or values me."

"I'll always be alone."

"I don't deserve a loving family or partner."

Alright, let's dig a little deeper. What negative self-talk have you caught yourself saying or heard others say? This is your chance to confront those limiting beliefs head-on. Jot down your thoughts right here, or flip to the extra pages at the end of the book to really dive in. You got this—let's keep winning and turning those negative thoughts into positive vibes. God bless.

....

....

....

....

....

Reflection Questions

"What actions can I take today to show my loved ones I care?"

"How can I practice patience and understanding in challenging situations?"

"What past hurts or misunderstandings do I need to let go of for my relationships to thrive?"

"How can I ensure I'm present and engaged in interacting with loved ones?"

"What does unconditional love mean to me, and how can I embody it daily?"

Dive into these reflection questions and let your thoughts flow. Whether you jot down your answers right here or flip to the extra pages at the end of the book, make this space your own. You got this—let's keep winning. God bless.

....

....

....

....

....

....

....

....

....

....

Family and Love

STEPS NO.	STEPS	DESCRIPTION &EXAMPLES
Step 1	Identify Negative Self-Talk or Actions	Recognize the negative self-talk or actions that are affecting your relationships and family life. **Example:** "I'm not a good enough parent/spouse.
Step 2	Trace the Root Cause	Dig deep to find the root cause of this negative self-talk or action. Is it past experiences, societal expectations, or something else? **Example:** "I feel inadequate because I can't spend enough time with my family due to work.
Step 3	Challenge and Reframe	Challenge these negative thoughts. Are they based on facts or assumptions? Reframe them into neutral or positive statements. **Example:** "I may be busy, but that doesn't make me a bad parent/spouse. I can find quality time to spend with my family.
Step 4	Implement Positive Affirmations	Replace the negative self-talk with positive affirmations tailored to your family and love life. **Example:** "I am a loving and caring parent/spouse. My family understands and supports me. Let's keep winning in love and family!"
Step 5	Monitor and Celebrate	Implement actionable steps to align your behavior with your new positive mindset. **Example:** "I will schedule regular family time and be fully present during those moments."

Positive Affirmations / Self-Talk for "Family & Love"

1. *"Family is the compass that guides me. God bless its unbreakable bond."*

2. *"Love in our home is the strongest foundation. We're built on it."*

3. *"Every day, I cherish the moments with my loved ones."*

4. *"Let's keep winning as a family, supporting and uplifting each other."*

5. *"In our family, love knows no bounds. It's infinite and eternal."*

6. *"Challenges only make our family bond stronger. We got this!"*

7. *"God's love reflects in every family member."*

8. *"Every day, I'm grateful for the love surrounding me."*

9. *"Our family is a circle of strength and love; with every challenge faced, it grows."*

10. *"Love, patience, and faith are the pillars of our family."*

11. *"Together as a family, we create countless love-filled memories."*

12. *"I am blessed with a family that stands by me, no matter what."*

13. *"Every family gathering is a reminder of God's grace."*

14. *"Let's keep winning in love and understanding every single day."*

15. *"In our home, every laughter and tear strengthens our bond."*

16. *"Family is where life begins, and love never ends."*

17. *"I am committed to nurturing, loving, and protecting my family."*

18. *"God bless the hands that support, the hearts that love, and the souls that uplift in our family."*

19. *"Our family's love story is my favorite."*

20. *"Every day, I am inspired by the love and strength of my family."*

21. *"In our family, every challenge is met with love and faith."*

22. *"God's blessings are evident in the love we share as a family."*

23. *"Let's keep winning in understanding, patience, and love."*

24. *"The love in our family flows strong and deep, leaving us memories to treasure and keep."*

25. *"Every moment with my family is a reminder of God's endless love."*

26. *"Together, we are a family, bound by love and trust."*

27. *"Our family is a beautiful blend of love, laughter, and grace."*

28. *"God bless our family with unity, love, and understanding."*

29. *"In our family, love doesn't divide; it multiplies."*

30. *"Let's keep winning in creating loving memories as a family."*

31. *"Every day, I am grateful for the love that binds our family."*

32. *"Our family is a testament to God's love and blessings."*

33. *"In love and unity, our family stands unshaken."*

34. *"God's love shines brightest in the heart of our family."*

35. *"Every challenge faced together makes our family love grow deeper."*

36. *"Let's keep winning and cherishing every moment as a family."*

37. *"The love within our family is a beacon of hope and strength."*

38. *"God bless every laughter, tear, and memory shared in our family."*

39. *"Our family is where love is endless and memories are timeless."*

40. *"In our family, every member is a unique expression of God's love."*

41. *"Let's keep winning in nurturing and supporting each other."*

42. *"The foundation of our family is built on trust, love, and faith."*

43. *"God's grace is evident in the unity of our family."*

44. *"Every day, I am inspired to love deeper, thanks to my family."*

45. *"In our family, every challenge is an opportunity to grow in love."*

46. *"Let's keep winning in patience, understanding, and compassion."*

47. *"The love in our family is a legacy passed down through generations."*

48. *"God bless the bond that keeps our family united."*

49. *"Our family is a tapestry of love, woven with memories and blessings."*

50. *"In our family, love is the strongest currency."*

51. *"Let's keep winning in creating a legacy of love for generations to come."*

52. *"Every meal shared, every prayer said, strengthens our family bond."*

53. *"God's love is the glue that binds our family together."*

54. *"In our family, every day is a celebration of love and togetherness."*

55. *"Challenges are stepping stones to a stronger family bond."*

56. *"Let's keep winning in faith, hope, and love."*

57. *"The love in our family is a reflection of God's eternal love."*

58. *"Every moment spent with family is a treasure."*

59. *"God bless our family's journey, filled with love and memories."*

60. *"Our family is a circle of love, unbroken by time or distance."*

61. *"Let's keep winning in cherishing, nurturing, and loving."*

62. *"In our family, every member is a beacon of love and hope."*

63. *"God's blessings shine brightest in the heart of our home."*

64. *"The love we share as a family is our greatest strength."*

65. *"Every challenge faced together is a testament to our family's love."*

66. *"Let's keep winning in understanding, supporting, and cherishing."*

67. *"Our family is a haven of love, trust, and faith."*

68. *"God bless the love that binds, the hands that support, and the hearts that cherish in our family."*

69. *"In our family, love is the language spoken by all."*

70. *"Every memory created as a family is a page in our love story."*

71. *"Let's keep winning in creating moments of love and joy."*

72. *"The strength of our family lies in the love we share."*

73. *"God's grace is the foundation of our family's love."*

74. *"In our family, every day is a testament to love's power."*

75. *"Challenges are moments that enrich our family's love story."*

76. *"Let's keep winning in faith, love, and unity."*

77. *"Our family is where love finds its truest expression."*

78. *"God bless the journey, the love, and the memories of our family."*

79. *"In our family, love is the thread that binds us together."*

80. *"Every challenge, every joy shared, deepens our family bond."*

81. *"Let's keep winning in cherishing every blessing as a family."*

82. *"The love in our family is a legacy of blessings and memories."*

83. *"God's love is the guiding light in our family's journey."*

84. *"In our family, love is the anchor that holds us together."*

85. *"Every moment, every memory is a testament to our family's love."*

86. *"Let's keep winning in nurturing, supporting, and understanding."*

87. *"Our family is a tapestry of God's love, woven with blessings."*

88. *"God bless the love, the unity, and the strength of our family."*

89. *"In our family, love is the compass that guides us."*

90. *"Every challenge faced is a chapter in our family's love story."*

91. *"Let's keep winning in faith, hope, and endless love."*

92. *"The love we share as a family is God's greatest gift to us."*

93. *"God's blessings are the foundation of our family's love story."*

94. *"In our family, love is the melody that soothes every heart."*

95. *"Every memory, every moment is a testament to our family's love."*

96. *"Let's keep winning in cherishing, loving, and supporting."*

97. *"Our family is where God's love finds its truest expression."*

98. *"God bless the bond, the love, and the memories of our family."*

99. *"In our family, love is the bridge that connects every heart."*

100. *"Every challenge, every joy is a page in our family's love story."*

101. *"Let's keep winning in faith, unity, and endless love."*

102. *"The love in our family is a beacon of hope and strength."*

103. *"God's grace is the melody that sings in our family's heart."*

104. *"In our family, love is the anchor, the strength, and the guide."*

105. *"Every memory, every challenge is a testament to our family's love."*

106. *"Let's keep winning in cherishing, nurturing, and understanding."*

107. *"Our family is a circle of God's love, unbroken and eternal."*

108. *"God bless the journey, the challenges, and the love of our family."*

109. *"In our family, love is the compass, the guide, and the destination."*

110. *"Every moment, every challenge deepens our family's bond of love."*

111. *"Let's keep winning in faith, love, and cherished memories."*

112. *"The love we share as a family is God's blessing in its truest form."*

113. *"God's grace is the foundation, the strength of our family's love."*

114. *"In our family, love is the melody, the song, and the dance."*

115. *"Every challenge, every joy is a chapter in our family's love story."*

116. *"Let's keep winning in unity, understanding, and endless love."*

117. *"Our family is where God's love shines brightest."*

118. *"God bless the bond, the unity, and the love of our family."*

119. *"In our family, love is the anchor, the guide, and the journey."*

120. *"Every memory, every challenge is a testament to our family's love."*

121. *"Let's keep winning in cherishing, supporting, and loving."*

122. *"The love in our family is a legacy, a blessing, and a journey."*

123. *"God's grace is the melody, the song of our family's heart."*

124. *"In our family, love is the compass, the guide, and the light."*

125. *"Every challenge, every joy deepens our family's bond of love."*

126. *"Let's keep winning in faith, unity, and cherished memories."*

127. *"Our family is a circle of God's love, eternal and unbroken."*

128. *"God bless the journey, the love, and the memories of our family."*

129. *"In our family, love is the bridge, the anchor, and the guide."*

130. *"Every moment, every challenge is a chapter in our family's love story."*

131. *"Let's keep winning in cherishing, nurturing, and understanding."*

132. *"The love we share as a family is God's greatest gift to us."*

133. "God's blessings are the foundation of our family's love story."

134. "In our family, love is the melody that soothes every soul."

135. "Every memory, every moment is a testament to our family's love."

136. "Let's keep winning in faith, hope, and endless love."

137. "Our family is where God's love finds its truest expression."

138. "God bless the bond, the love, and the unity of our family."

139. "In our family, love is the compass that guides every heart."

140. "Every challenge faced is a testament to our family's love."

141. "Let's keep winning in cherishing, loving, and supporting."

142. "Our family is a tapestry of God's love, woven with blessings."

143. "God's love is the guiding light in our family's journey."

144. "In our family, love is the anchor that holds every heart."

145. "Every moment, every memory is a testament to our family's love."

146. "Let's keep winning in nurturing, supporting, and cherishing."

147. "The love in our family is a legacy of blessings and memories."

148. "God bless the journey, the love, and the unity of our family."

149. "In our family, love is the language spoken by every heart."

150. "Every challenge, every joy is a testament to our family's unbreakable bond of love."

Remember, Family is where love begins and never ends. In the journey of life, relationships are the treasures we gather. Cherish them, nurture them, and let love be your guiding light. Let's keep winning in love, unity, and faith. You got this. God bless.

Health & Well-being

"The greatest wealth is health."
- Virgil

"It is health that is real wealth and not pieces of gold and silver."
- Mahatma Gandhi

"Your body hears everything your mind says."
- Naomi Judd

"He who has health has hope, and he who has hope has everything."
- Arabian Proverb

"To keep the body in good health is a duty, otherwise we shall not be able to keep our mind strong and clear."
- Buddha

The Garden of Life: Nurturing Your Divine Health

In the 21st century, where technology reigns supreme, and convenience is king, our health and well-being often take a backseat. But what if we looked at our bodies and minds as sacred gardens, gifts from the Divine, waiting to be nurtured and cherished?

John was a tech-savvy entrepreneur, always on the move, grabbing fast food on the go and burning the midnight oil. His life was a whirlwind of meetings, deadlines, and digital screens. But one day, he stumbled upon a forgotten passage from the Bible, "*Your body is a temple of the Holy Spirit*" (1 Corinthians 6:19). It struck a chord. Inspired, John decided to transform his city balcony into a small garden. As he planted seeds and watched them grow, he drew parallels with his health. Just as the plants needed sunlight, water, and care, his body and mind required proper nutrition, rest, and positive affirmations. One day, as he watered his plants, he remembered the biblical story of the Garden of Eden, a place of harmony, abundance, and well-being. He realized he could also create his own Eden by making conscious choices for his health and well-being. With this newfound revelation, John began his mornings with affirmations:

"My body is a divine temple; I nourish it with love and care."

"Every cell in my body vibrates with energy and health."

"I am in harmony with nature and listen to its wisdom."

"Let's keep winning, for my health is my wealth."

"I got this, for the Divine guides my choices and blesses my well-being."

John shared his journey with friends and family. He advised them to see health not just as a physical state but as a spiritual journey. "*Connect with nature, even if it's a plant on your windowsill. Listen to your body, rest when needed, and feed it with foods that heal and nourish. Remember, just as a garden thrives with care, so does your body with love and attention.*"

Months into his journey, John felt rejuvenated. He took moments to sit in his balcony garden, reflecting on his progress, his choices, and the divine guidance that led him to honor his body and mind. He realized that health wasn't just about the absence of disease but the presence of holistic well-being.

Examples of Negative Self-Talk for "Health & Well-being"

"I'll never be fit or healthy."

"Why bother eating right? It doesn't make a difference."

"I'm just naturally prone to illness."

"I don't have the willpower to maintain a healthy lifestyle."

"I hate how I look and feel."

"It's too late for me to make health changes."

"I don't deserve to feel good or be healthy."

"I'll never be as healthy as others."

"I'm just not strong enough to resist temptations."

"Being healthy is too hard and not worth the effort."

Alright, let's dig a little deeper. What negative self-talk have you caught yourself saying or heard others say? This is your chance to confront those limiting beliefs head-on. Jot down your thoughts right here, or flip to the extra pages at the end of the book to really dive in. You got this—let's keep winning and turning those negative thoughts into positive vibes. God bless.

....

....

....

....

....

Reflection Questions

"What does 'health' mean to me, and how does it align with my spiritual beliefs?"

"What small step can I take today to nurture my 'garden' of well-being?"

"How do my daily choices reflect the value I place on my health?"

"When was the last time I truly felt vibrant and alive, and what contributed to that feeling?"

"What positive affirmations can I incorporate daily to foster a mindset of health and abundance?"

Dive into these reflection questions and let your thoughts flow. Whether you jot down your answers right here or flip to the extra pages at the end of the book, make this space your own. You got this—let's keep winning. God bless.

....

....

....

....

....

....

....

....

....

Health & Well-being

STEPS	BOX LABEL	DESCRIPTION &EXAMPLES
Step 1	**Recognize Negative Self-Talk or Actions**	The first step is to become aware of any negative self-talk or actions that don't align with your health and well-being goals. **Examples:** "I'll never be fit," "Eating junk food," "Skipping workouts"
Step 2	**Find the Root Cause**	Dig deeper to understand the underlying reasons for the negative self-talk or actions. **Examples:** Fear of failure, past experiences, societal pressures.
Step 3	**Challenge and Reframe Negative Thoughts**	Actively question the validity of your negative thoughts and reframe them into positive affirmations. **Examples:** Change "I'll never be fit" to "Every day, I am getting healthier and stronger."
Step 4	**Take Positive Actions**	Replace negative actions with positive habits that align with your health and well-being goals. **Examples:** Choose a salad over junk food, go for a 20-minute walk, practice mindfulness.
Step 5	**Monitor and Celebrate**	Keep track of your progress and celebrate small wins to reinforce your new positive habits. **Examples:** Kept a food journal, completed a week of workouts, felt more energized.

Positive Affirmations / Self-Talk for "Health & Well-being"

1. "Every cell in my body vibrates with energy and health. Let's keep winning!"

2. "I am whole, strong, and vibrant. God's got my back!"

3. "Every day, in every way, I am getting healthier and stronger."

4. "I honor my body and treat it with respect."

5. "God's love heals me, inside and out."

6. "I deserve a healthy, happy life."

7. "My body is a temple; I treat it with love and care."

8. "I am surrounded by healing energy every moment."

9. "I trust my body's natural ability to heal itself."

10. "Every breath I take fills me with peace and vitality."

11. "I am in tune with my body's needs and desires."

12. "I am in control of my health and wellness."

13. "I choose habits that promote my well-being."

14. "I am resilient, strong, and brave."

15. "I release all illness, pain, and discomfort. They have no place in my life."

16. "I am blessed with a robust immune system."

17. "Every meal I eat nourishes my body and soul."

18. "I am grateful for the health and vitality that flows through me."

19. "I am in perfect health, mind, body, and spirit."

20. "I radiate good health."

21. "My body knows how to heal, and I support it in doing so."

22. "I am surrounded by people who encourage and support my healthy choices."

23. "I am full of energy and vitality."

24. "I listen to my body and give it what it needs."

25. "I am free from pain and discomfort."

26. "I am strong, fit, and healthy."

27. "I am in control of my well-being."

28. "I am blessed with a body that serves me well."

29. "I am worthy of living a healthy life."

30. "I am in harmony with my body."

31. "I am constantly discovering new ways to improve my health."

32. "I am grateful for the healing that's happening in my body right now."

33. "I am in love with taking care of my body."

34. "I deserve a body that functions perfectly."

35. "I am the picture of good health and vitality."

36. "I am in charge of my health."

37. "I am filled with gratitude for the health that I enjoy."

38. "I am free from sickness."

39. "I am always guided to make healthy choices."

40. "I am blessed with a strong and healthy body."

41. "I am constantly rejuvenated by divine health."

42. *"I am in sync with my body's rhythms."*

43. *"I am the master of my body and health."*

44. *"I am surrounded by healing light."*

45. *"I am focused on healing and wellness."*

46. *"I am committed to living a healthy lifestyle."*

47. *"I am in perfect health and filled with gratitude."*

48. *"I am nourished by the foods I eat."*

49. *"I am a beacon of health and well-being."*

50. *"I am in tune with my body's needs."*

51. *"I am the embodiment of health."*

52. *"I am constantly revitalized by divine energy."*

53. *"I deserve a life free from pain and suffering."*

54. *"I am in control of my health and wellness journey."*

55. *"I am blessed with a body that heals quickly."*

56. *"I am committed to treating my body with love and respect."*

57. *"I am in harmony with my body's natural rhythms."*

58. *"I am filled with energy every single day."*

59. *"I am grateful for the strength and health of my body."*

60. *"I am constantly surrounded by healing energy."*

61. *"I am the master of my body."*

62. *"I am filled with vitality."*

63. *"I am in charge of my health journey."*

64. *"I am blessed with a body that serves me in all ways."*

65. *"I am constantly rejuvenated."*

66. *"I am the picture of health and vitality."*

67. *"I am committed to nurturing my body."*

68. *"I am in love with my healthy body."*

69. *"I am always guided to make the best decisions for my health."*

70. *"I am a magnet for health and well-being."*

71. *"I am constantly revitalized by divine love."*

72. *"I am in harmony with my body's needs."*

73. *"I am the embodiment of vitality."*

74. *"I am in control of my health destiny."*

75. *"I am blessed with robust health."*

76. *"I am committed to living a life of health and wellness."*

77. *"I am in tune with my body's wisdom."*

78. *"I am a beacon of vitality."*

79. *"I am the master of my health destiny."*

80. *"I am constantly surrounded by love and healing."*

81. *"I am in charge of my body and health."*

82. *"I am blessed with a life of health and well-being."*

83. *"I am the picture of vitality."*

84. *"I am in love with my body, and all it does for me."*

85. *"I am always guided to the best choices for my health."*

86. *"I am a magnet for vitality and well-being."*

87. *"I am constantly rejuvenated by divine vitality."*

88. *"I am in harmony with my body's natural healing processes."*

89. *"I am the embodiment of well-being."*

90. *"I am in control of my health and life."*

91. *"I am blessed with a body in perfect health."*

92. *"I am committed to nurturing and caring for my body."*

93. *"I am in love with the vitality that flows through me."*

94. *"I am always making the best choices for my health."*

95. *"I am a beacon of well-being and vitality."*

96. *"I am the master of my body and well-being."*

97. *"I am constantly surrounded by healing and love."*

98. *"I am in charge of my health journey and destiny."*

99. *"I am blessed with a life of vitality and health."*

100. *"I am the picture of well-being and health."*

101. *"I am in love with the energy that flows through me."*

102. *"I am always guided to the best decisions for my well-being."*

103. *"I am a magnet for health and vitality."*

104. *"I am constantly rejuvenated by divine well-being."*

105. *"I am in harmony with my body's natural rhythms and cycles."*

106. *"I am the embodiment of health and vitality."*

107. *"I am in control of my well-being and my destiny."*

108. *"I am blessed with robust health and vitality."*

109. *"I am committed to living a life of vitality and health."*

110. *"I am in tune with my body's natural healing abilities."*

111. *"I am a beacon of health and well-being."*

112. *"I am the master of my health and my vitality."*

113. *"I am constantly surrounded by love and vitality."*

114. *"I am in charge of my health and life's journey."*

115. *"I am blessed with a life of health and vitality."*

116. *"I am the picture of health and well-being."*

117. *"I am in love with the vitality and energy in me."*

118. *"I am always making the best choices for my well-being."*

119. *"I am a magnet for health and well-being."*

120. *"I am constantly rejuvenated by divine health."*

121. *"I am in harmony with my body's needs and desires."*

122. *"I am the embodiment of vitality and health."*

123. *"I am in control of my well-being and life's journey."*

124. *"I am blessed with a body in perfect health and vitality."*

125. *"I am committed to nurturing and caring for my body and mind."*

126. *"I am in love with the health and vitality in me."*

127. *"I am always guided to the best decisions for my health and well-being."*

128. *"I am a beacon of vitality and health."*

129. *"I am the master of my body and my health."*

130. *"I am constantly surrounded by healing, love, and vitality."*

131. *"I am in charge of my health and my destiny."*

132. *"I am blessed with a life of health, vitality, and well-being."*

133. *"I am the picture of vitality and well-being."*

134. *"I am in love with the energy and vitality that flows through me."*

135. *"I am always making the best choices for my health and vitality."*

136. *"I am a magnet for vitality and health."*

137. *"I am constantly rejuvenated by divine love and health."*

138. *"I am in harmony with my body's natural healing processes."*

139. *"I am the embodiment of health and well-being."*

140. *"I am in control of my health and life's journey."*

141. *"I am blessed with a body that serves me in health and vitality."*

142. *"I am committed to living a life of health, vitality, and well-being."*

143. *"I am in tune with my body's wisdom and guidance."*

144. *"I am a beacon of health, vitality, and well-being."*

145. *"I am the master of my health, body, and destiny."*

146. *"I am constantly surrounded by love, healing, and vitality."*

147. *"I am in charge of my health, well-being, and life."*

148. *"I am blessed with a life of health, well-being, and vitality."*

149. *"I am the picture of health, vitality, and well-being."*

150. *"I am in love with the health, vitality, and well-being within me. Let's keep winning!"*

Your Health is your wealth. Nurture it, cherish it, and let it shine. Let's keep winning in the garden of life. You got this. God bless.

Mindfulness & Focus

"The present moment is the only moment available to us."
- Thich Nhat Hanh

"Wherever you are, be there totally."
- Eckhart Tolle

"The best way to capture moments is to pay attention."
- Jon Kabat-Zinn

"In today's rush, we all think too much and feel too little."
- Charlie Chaplin

"The future is always beginning now."
- Mark Strand

The Still Waters of the Digital Age

In our world, where the hum of technology is constant and the glow of screens ever-present, the concept of mindfulness and focus seems almost archaic. Yet, it's in these ancient principles, rooted deeply in biblical teachings, that we find the antidote to our modern-day distractions.

James was a tech-savvy millennial, always connected, always online. His day began with checking notifications and ended with scrolling through endless feeds. But amidst this digital chaos, he felt a void, a lack of connection not to the world, but to himself. One day, while reading the Bible, he came across Psalm 23: *"He leads me beside still waters; He restores my soul."* It struck a chord. The still waters, he realized, were a metaphor for a state of mindfulness, focused tranquility amidst life's storms. Inspired, James decided to embark on a journey of mindfulness. He began with small steps, like meditating for five minutes daily, focusing solely on his breath. Over time, he introduced more practices, drawing inspiration from biblical teachings. Each morning, as the sun's first rays painted the sky, James would sit in quiet reflection, affirming:

1. *"In this moment, I am present. I am at peace."*

2. *"The still waters of God's grace flow through me, bringing clarity and focus."*

3. *"I am divinely guided in every action I take."*

4. *"Let's keep winning, for every breath I take is a testament to God's grace."*

5. *"Distractions do not define me; my divine purpose does."*

James began sharing his journey with friends, advising them on the importance of mindfulness in the digital age. "*It's not about shunning technology,*" he'd say, "*but about using it mindfully. Set boundaries. Dedicate moments in your day where you connect with yourself, with God. Remember, in stillness, we find clarity. You got this.*"

Months turned into years, and James's commitment to mindfulness transformed not just his daily routine but his very essence. He often reflected on his growth, the serenity he felt, and the deeper connection he had forged with God. He realized that in the still waters of mindfulness, he had found his anchor, his true north.

Examples of Negative Self-Talk for "Mindfulness & Focus"

"I can't concentrate on anything."

"My mind is always scattered."

"I'm just not the meditative type."

"I'll never find peace in this chaos."

"I'm too busy to be mindful."

"I've tried focusing, but it's just not for me."

"I'm always going to be distracted."

"Mindfulness is for monks, not for someone like me."

"I don't have the patience to be still."

"I can't control my wandering thoughts."

Alright, let's dig a little deeper. What negative self-talk have you caught yourself saying or heard others say? This is your chance to confront those limiting beliefs head-on. Jot down your thoughts right here, or flip to the extra pages at the end of the book to really dive in. You got this—let's keep winning and turning those negative thoughts into positive vibes. God bless.

....

....

....

....

....

Reflection Questions

"When was the last time I truly felt present in a moment, and what was I doing?"

"How does my constant connectivity impact my mental and emotional well-being?"

"What small step can I take today to introduce mindfulness into my routine?"

"How does my current state of focus align with my divine purpose?"

"What distractions can I eliminate to pave the way for a more focused and mindful tomorrow?"

Dive into these reflection questions and let your thoughts flow. Whether you jot down your answers right here or flip to the extra pages at the end of the book, make this space your own. You got this—let's keep winning. God bless.

....

....

....

....

....

....

....

....

....

Mindfulness and Focus

STEPS	BOX LABEL	DESCRIPTION &EXAMPLES
Step 1	**Negative Self-Talk or Actions**	Recognize the negative self-talk or actions that are hindering your mindfulness and focus. **Examples:** "I can't concentrate," "Mindfulness is a waste of time," "I'm too busy to focus."
Step 2	**Root Cause Analysis**	Dig deep to find the root cause of this negative self-talk or action. **Examples:** Stress, past failures, societal beliefs.
Step 3	**Challenge & Reframe**	Challenge these negative thoughts or actions and reframe them with positive affirmations. **Examples:** "I have the power to focus," "Mindfulness enriches my life."
Step 4	**New Habits for Mindfulness & Focus**	Develop new habits that align with your reframed thoughts to improve mindfulness and focus. **Examples:** Daily meditation, time-blocking for tasks, mindful breathing.
Step 5	**Monitor & Adjust**	Keep track of your progress. Make adjustments as needed to maintain improved mindfulness and focus. **Examples:** Weekly reflection, journaling, or discussing progress with a mentor.

Positive Affirmations / Self-Talk for "Mindfulness & Focus"

1. *"Today, I am fully present in every moment."*

2. *"Every breath I take centers me more and more."*

3. *"I am in tune with the universe and its rhythm."*

4. *"Mindfulness is the key to my inner peace."*

5. *"I am focused, alert, and attentive right now."*

6. *"Every task I take on, I do with full intention."*

7. *"I let go of distractions and embrace clarity."*

8. *"The universe supports my journey to mindfulness."*

9. *"I am grounded in this moment, and it's beautiful."*

10. *"With every inhale, I draw in focus. With every exhale, I release chaos."*

11. *"I am in control of where my attention goes."*

12. *"Today, I choose to be fully engaged in my tasks."*

13. *"I am the master of my thoughts and focus."*

14. *"Every day, I grow in mindfulness and presence."*

15. *"I am attuned to my inner guidance."*

16. *"Distractions do not define me; my focus does."*

17. *"I am here, I am now, and I am free."*

18. *"The present moment is my true home."*

19. *"I cherish the beauty of now."*

20. *"Every moment is a gift, and I am grateful."*

21. *"I am centered, I am balanced, I am at peace."*

22. *"I find joy in the simplicity of the present."*

23. *"I am connected to the world around me."*

24. *"Mindfulness is my path to true happiness."*

25. *"I am in harmony with the now."*

26. *"With mindfulness, I transform every experience into wisdom."*

27. *"I am attuned to the whispers of the universe."*

28. *"Every moment is an opportunity for mindfulness."*

29. *"I am a beacon of focus and clarity."*

30. *"I embrace the journey of being fully present."*

31. *"I am anchored in the beauty of the present moment."*

32. *"Every day, I cultivate a deeper sense of focus."*

33. *"I am in sync with the rhythm of life."*

34. *"I am mindful, I am grateful, I am blessed."*

35. *"Today, I choose mindfulness over chaos."*

36. *"I am the captain of my focus."*

37. *"I am deeply connected to this very moment."*

38. *"With every heartbeat, I am more and more present."*

39. *"I celebrate the power of now."*

40. *"I am a magnet for focus and clarity."*

41. *"I am fully immersed in the beauty of this moment."*

42. *"I am the embodiment of mindfulness."*

43. *"I am in a sacred partnership with the present."*

44. *"Every second is a canvas, and I paint it with mindfulness."*

45. *"I am in a dance with the universe, here and now."*

46. *"I am a warrior of focus and determination."*

47. *"I am in a loving relationship with the present moment."*

48. *"I am the master of my mind and focus."*

49. *"I am on a sacred journey of mindfulness."*

50. *"I am in tune with the melody of the present."*

51. *"I am a beacon of mindfulness in a chaotic world."*

52. *"I am the architect of my focus."*

53. *"I am in a symphony with the now."*

54. *"I am a vessel of peace and presence."*

55. *"I am on a pilgrimage to the heart of the present moment."*

56. *"I am the guardian of my attention."*

57. *"I am in a sacred communion with the now."*

58. *"I am the champion of my focus."*

59. *"I am in a dance with the divine, here and now."*

60. *"I am a fortress of mindfulness and clarity."*

61. *"I am in a romance with the present moment."*

62. *"I am the commander of my attention."*

63. *"I am in a serenade with the now."*

64. *"I am a sanctuary of peace and presence."*

65. *"I am on a quest for the beauty of the present."*

66. *"I am the custodian of my focus."*

67. *"I am in a duet with the divine, here and now."*

68. *"I am a citadel of mindfulness."*

69. *"I am in a ballet with the universe in this moment."*

70. *"I am the steward of my attention."*

71. *"I am in a waltz with the world, here and now."*

72. *"I am a haven of peace and presence."*

73. *"I am on a voyage to the soul of the present moment."*

74. *"I am the caretaker of my focus."*

75. *"I am in a tango with time, here and now."*

76. *"I am a refuge of mindfulness and clarity."*

77. *"I am on a journey to the essence of the present."*

78. *"I am the guardian of my mind."*

79. *"I am in a symphony with the seconds, here and now."*

80. *"I am a bastion of peace and presence."*

81. *"I am on an odyssey to the heart of the now."*

82. *"I am the protector of my focus."*

83. *"I am in a melody with the minutes, here and now."*

84. *"I am a stronghold of mindfulness."*

85. *"I am on a trek to the spirit of the present moment."*

86. *"I am the sentinel of my attention."*

87. *"I am in harmony with the hours, here and now."*

88. *"I am a fortress of peace and presence."*

89. *"I am on a trip to the core of the now."*

90. *"I am the watchman of my focus."*

91. "I am in a rhythm with the days, here and now."

92. "I am a tower of mindfulness and clarity."

93. "I am on a path to the pulse of the present."

94. "I am the overseer of my attention."

95. "I am in a beat with the weeks, here and now."

96. "I am a pillar of peace and presence."

97. "I am on a route to the rhythm of the now."

98. "I am the supervisor of my focus."

99. "I am in a cadence with the months, here and now."

100. "I am a monument of mindfulness."

101. "Let's keep winning by embracing the present."

102. "Every moment is a gift, and I am here to unwrap it."

103. "I am the beacon guiding my focus."

104. "I am in a dance with destiny, here and now."

105. "I am a temple of peace and presence."

106. "Every second is sacred, and I honor it."

107. "I am the lighthouse shining light on my attention."

108. "I am in a duet with destiny, here and now."

109. "I am a shrine of mindfulness and clarity."

110. "Every minute is a miracle, and I am here to witness it."

111. "I am the torch illuminating my focus."

112. "I am in a ballet with blessings, here and now."

113. "I am a chapel of peace and presence."

114. *"Every hour is holy, and I am here to honor it."*

115. *"I am the flame fueling my attention."*

116. *"I am in a tango with timelessness, here and now."*

117. *"I am a sanctuary of mindfulness."*

118. *"Every day is divine, and I am here to delight in it."*

119. *"I am the spark igniting my focus."*

120. *"I am in a waltz with wonder, here and now."*

121. *"I am a cathedral of peace and presence."*

122. *"Every week is wondrous, and I am here to welcome it."*

123. *"I am the star steering my attention."*

124. *"I am in a rhythm with reverence, here and now."*

125. *"I am a mosque of mindfulness and clarity."*

126. *"Every month is magical, and I am here to marvel at it."*

127. *"I am the sun shining on my focus."*

128. *"I am in a beat with blessings, here and now."*

129. *"I am a pagoda of peace and presence."*

130. *"Every year is a blessing, and I am here to behold it."*

131. *"I am the moon molding my attention."*

132. *"I am in a cadence with the cosmos, here and now."*

133. *"I am a synagogue of mindfulness."*

134. *"Every decade is divine, and I am here to dance in it."*

135. *"I am the comet charting my focus."*

136. *"I am in a melody with miracles, here and now."*

137. *"I am a temple of tranquility."*

138. *"Every century is sacred, and I am here to savor it."*

139. *"I am the galaxy guiding my attention."*

140. *"I am in harmony with the heavens, here and now."*

141. *"I am a universe of understanding."*

142. *"Every millennium is a miracle, and I am here to muse on it."*

143. *"I am the cosmos channeling my focus."*

144. *"I am in a symphony with the stars, here and now."*

145. *"I am a realm of reverence."*

146. *"Every eon is eternal, and I am here to embrace it."*

147. *"I am the infinity inspiring my attention."*

148. *"I am in a rhythm with the realms, here and now."*

149. *"I am a dimension of divinity."*

150. *"Every moment is eternal, and I am here, fully present, fully alive. Let's keep winning."*

Life's true essence is in being present, in embracing the now. Dive deep, reflect, and find that inner peace within. In the hustle and bustle of our digital age, finding our still waters might seem challenging. But remember, with faith and focus, we can navigate any storm. You got this. Let's keep winning. God bless.

Professional Success

"Success usually comes to those who are too busy to be looking for it."
- Henry David Thoreau

"Opportunities don't happen. You create them."
- Chris Grosser

"Success is not just about making money. It's about making a difference."
- *Kathy Calvin*

"Success is the sum of small efforts, repeated day in and day out."
- Robert Collier

"Don't watch the clock; do what it does. Keep going."
- Sam Levenson

The Story of the Modern-Day David: Climbing the Corporate Goliath

Today, the battlefield isn't a vast open space with warriors but the corporate world, filled with challenges, competition, and the constant quest for success. The Goliaths today aren't giants of flesh and bone but towering obstacles of self-doubt, societal expectations, and professional setbacks. But remember, every Goliath has a David, and every challenge has a solution rooted in faith, determination, and the right mindset.

Michael was a young professional, fresh out of college, stepping into the corporate world with dreams in his eyes. But soon, he realized that this world was filled with Goliath's - colleagues who doubted him, projects that seemed insurmountable, and a nagging voice inside that whispered he wasn't good enough. One evening, feeling particularly low after a challenging meeting, Michael stumbled upon his childhood Bible. A story he had heard countless times as a child caught his eye - the tale of David and Goliath. With unwavering faith in God and a simple sling, the young shepherd boy defeated the mighty giant. Inspired, Michael decided to tackle his professional challenges head-on. He began to see every setback as an opportunity, every doubter as a motivator, and every failure as a stepping stone. With faith as his sling, he aimed for the stars. Every morning, before stepping into the office, Michael would recite:

1. *"I am equipped with the strength and wisdom of the Divine to face any challenge."*

2. *"Every Goliath in my path is an opportunity for growth."*

3. *"I deserve success, and I work with integrity and passion."*

4. "Let's keep winning, for with God by my side, no obstacle is too big."

5. "I got this, for the same God that guided the shepherd boy guides me."

Michael's transformation didn't go unnoticed. Young interns and even seasoned colleagues would often seek his advice. He'd always say, *"Your faith is your sling, and your determination, your stone. Aim true, believe in yourself, and remember, every Goliath can be defeated."* He emphasized the importance of continuous learning, seeking mentorship, and, above all, never losing faith.

Years passed, and Michael climbed the corporate ladder, not by trampling others but by lifting them. He often took moments to reflect on his journey, the Goliaths he had faced, and the lessons each one taught him. He realized that true professional success wasn't just about titles or paychecks but about growth, integrity, and making a difference.

Negative Self-Talk for Professional Success

"I'm not cut out for this job."

"They probably think I'm a fraud."

"I'll never be as good as my colleagues."

"I'm bound to mess this up."

"Why did they even hire me?"

"I don't have the skills required for success."

"I'm just not leadership material."

"I'll never get that promotion."

"I'm out of my depth here."

"They're all judging my every move."

Alright, let's dig a little deeper. What negative self-talk have you caught yourself saying or heard others say? This is your chance to confront those limiting beliefs head-on. Jot down your thoughts right here, or flip to the extra pages at the end of the book to really dive in. You got this—let's keep winning and turning those negative thoughts into positive vibes. God bless.

....

....

....

....

....

Reflection Questions

"What Goliaths am I currently facing in my professional life, and how can I tackle them with faith and determination?"

"How do I define professional success, and is it aligned with my personal values and goals?"

"What skills or knowledge do I need to acquire to overcome my current challenges?"

"Who are the mentors or guides in my life that can provide wisdom and guidance?"

"How can I uplift others in my professional journey and create a positive impact?"

Dive into these reflection questions and let your thoughts flow. Whether you jot down your answers right here or flip to the extra pages at the end of the book, make this space your own. You got this—let's keep winning. God bless.

....

....

....

....

....

....

....

....

Professional Success

STEPS NO.	STEPS	DESCRIPTION &EXAMPLES
Step 1	Identify Negative Self-Talk or Actions	Recognize the negative self-talk or actions that are hindering your professional growth. **Example:** "I'm not good enough for that promotion" or procrastinating on important tasks.
Step 2	Trace the Root Cause	Dig deep to find the root cause of the negative self-talk or actions. Example: Fear of failure, imposter syndrome, or past experiences.
Step 3	Challenge and Reframe	Challenge the negative self-talk with evidence and reframe it into a positive affirmation. **Example:** "I have successfully led projects before, I am capable of earning that promotion."
Step 4	Take Actionable Steps	Identify and commit to actionable steps that align with your professional goals. **Example:** Update resume, take on additional responsibilities, or enroll in a skill-enhancing course.
Step 5	Establish New Habits	Consistently practice the positive affirmations and actions to establish new habits. **Example:** Daily affirmation practice, regular check-ins on project status, or setting aside time for skill development.

Positive Affirmations / Self-Talk for "Professional Success"

1. *"Every day, I'm stepping closer to my professional dreams."*

2. *"God has a plan for my career - it's more magnificent than I can imagine."*

3. *"I deserve every success that comes my way."*

4. *"Every challenge at work is an opportunity for growth."*

5. *"I am surrounded by opportunities. God bless each one."*

6. *"I've got the skills and the spirit to conquer any professional mountain."*

7. *"Every meeting, every project, every email is a step towards my success."*

8. *"I am a magnet for professional opportunities and growth."*

9. *"God's favor surrounds my career like a shield."*

10. *"I am resilient, strong, and destined for greatness in my profession."*

11. *"Every setback is a setup for a greater comeback. Let's keep winning!"*

12. *"I am blessed with a career that aligns with my purpose."*

13. *"I am constantly evolving and improving in my professional journey."*

14. *"Success is not just about making money; it's about making a difference."*

15. *"I am a leader, a game-changer, and a force to be reckoned with."*

16. *"Every day, I am inspired to bring my best self to work."*

17. *"I am surrounded by colleagues and mentors who uplift and inspire me."*

18. *"I am in charge of my professional destiny."*

19. *"God bless my hustle, my grind, and my vision."*

20. *"I am more than capable of achieving all my professional goals."*

21. *"Every project I touch turns to gold."*

22. *"I am constantly attracting new opportunities and challenges."*

23. *"I deserve promotions, raises, and every professional blessing."*

24. *"I am a beacon of inspiration and motivation at my workplace."*

25. *"I am always in the right place at the right time, professionally."*

26. *"I am blessed with a career that brings me joy and fulfillment."*

27. *"Every day, I progress towards my professional dreams."*

28. *"I am a powerhouse of ideas, innovation, and inspiration."*

29. *"God has equipped me with all the tools I need for professional success."*

30. *"I am constantly learning, growing, and evolving in my career."*

31. *"I am a magnet for success, prosperity, and professional growth."*

32. *"I deserve every accolade, every recognition, and every opportunity."*

33. *"I am a leader, a visionary, and a trailblazer in my field."*

34. *"I am constantly surrounded by opportunities to learn and grow."*

35. *"Every challenge is an opportunity in disguise. I've got this!"*

36. *"I am a vital asset to my organization and team."*

37. *"I am constantly inspired to bring innovative ideas to the table."*

38. *"I am blessed with a career that aligns with my passion and purpose."*

39. *"I am a beacon of positivity, motivation, and inspiration at work."*

40. *"I am always ahead of the curve, leading with vision and purpose."*

41. *"Every day, I am making strides towards my professional goals."*

42. *"I am a magnet for success, prosperity, and abundance in my career."*

43. *"I deserve every professional blessing that comes my way."*

44. *"I am a leader, a motivator, and a game-changer in my field."*

45. *"I am constantly surrounded by opportunities to excel and succeed."*

46. *"Every challenge is a steppingstone to greater success. Let's keep winning!"*

47. *"I am a vital asset to my team, my organization, and my industry."*

48. *"I am constantly inspired to innovate, create, and lead."*

49. *"I am blessed with a career that brings me joy, fulfillment, and success."*

50. *"I am a beacon of positivity, inspiration, and motivation in my profession."*

51. *"I am always in the right place at the right time, professionally speaking."*

52. *"I am a magnet for success, growth, and prosperity in my career."*

53. *"I deserve every accolade, every promotion, and every opportunity."*

54. *"I am a leader, a visionary, and a force to be reckoned with in my industry."*

55. *"I am surrounded by opportunities to learn, grow, and succeed."*

56. *"Every setback is a setup for a greater comeback in my career."*

57. *"I am a vital asset to my team, my organization, and my field."*

58. *"I am constantly inspired to bring fresh ideas and innovations to the table."*

59. *"I am blessed with a career that aligns with my passion and purpose."*

60. *"I am a beacon of positivity, motivation, and inspiration in my workplace."*

61. *"I am ahead of the game, leading with vision, purpose, and passion."*

62. *"Every day, I am making significant strides towards my professional goals."*

63. *"I am a magnet for success, abundance, and prosperity in my career."*

64. *"I deserve every professional blessing, opportunity, and recognition."*

65. *"I am a leader, a motivator, and a game-changer in my profession."*

66. *"I am constantly surrounded by opportunities to excel, grow, and lead."*

67. *"Every challenge is an opportunity for growth and success. I've got this!"*

68. *"I am a vital asset to my organization, my team, and my industry."*

69. *"I am constantly inspired to innovate, lead, and create in my field."*

70. *"I am blessed with a career that brings me immense joy, success, and fulfillment."*

71. *"I am a beacon of positivity, inspiration, and motivation in my profession."*

72. *"I am always in the right place at the right time for professional growth."*

73. *"I am a magnet for success, prosperity, and growth in my career."*

74. *"I deserve every accolade, every opportunity, and every blessing."*

75. *"I am a leader, a visionary, and a trailblazer in my profession."*

76. *"I am surrounded by opportunities to learn, excel, and succeed."*

77. *"Every setback is a setup for a professional comeback. Let's keep winning!"*

78. *"I am a vital asset to my team, my organization, and my field."*

79. *"I am inspired to bring innovative ideas and solutions to the table."*

80. *"I am blessed with a career that aligns with my passion and purpose."*

81. *"I am a beacon of positivity, motivation, and inspiration in my workplace."*

82. *"I am ahead of the curve, leading with vision, passion, and purpose."*

83. *"I am constantly making progress towards my professional dreams."*

84. *"I am a magnet for success, abundance, and prosperity in my career."*

85. *"I deserve every professional opportunity, recognition, and blessing."*

86. *"I am a leader, a motivator, and a force to be reckoned with in my field."*

87. *"I am constantly surrounded by opportunities to grow, lead, and excel."*

88. *"Every challenge is a steppingstone to greater success in my career."*

89. *"I am a vital asset to my organization, my team, and my profession."*

90. *"I am constantly inspired to innovate, create, and lead in my field."*

91. *"I am blessed with a career that brings me joy, success, and fulfillment."*

92. *"I am a beacon of positivity, inspiration, and motivation in my profession."*

93. *"I am in the right place at the right time for professional opportunities."*

94. *"I am a magnet for success, growth, and prosperity in my career."*

95. *"I deserve every accolade, every promotion, and every blessing."*

96. *"I am a leader, a visionary, and a game-changer in my profession."*

97. *"I am constantly surrounded by opportunities to excel, grow, and lead."*

98. *"Every setback is a setup for a greater comeback in my career. I've got this!"*

99. *"I am a vital asset to my team, my organization, and my industry."*

100. *"I am constantly inspired to bring fresh ideas and solutions to the table."*

101. "I am blessed with a career that aligns with my passion and purpose."

102. "I am a beacon of positivity, motivation, and inspiration in my workplace."

103. "I am ahead of the game, leading with vision, purpose, and passion."

104. "Every day, I progress towards my professional goals and dreams."

105. "I am a magnet for success, abundance, and prosperity in my career."

106. "I deserve every professional opportunity, accolade, and blessing."

107. "I am a leader, a motivator, and a force to be reckoned with in my field."

108. "I am surrounded by opportunities to learn, excel, and succeed."

109. "Every challenge is an opportunity for growth and success in my career."

110. "I am a vital asset to my organization, my team, and my profession."

111. "I am constantly inspired to innovate, lead, and create in my industry."

112. "I am blessed with a career that brings me immense joy, success, and fulfillment."

113. "I am a beacon of positivity, inspiration, and motivation in my profession."

114. "I am in the right place at the right time for professional growth."

115. "I am a magnet for success, prosperity, and growth in my career."

116. "I deserve every accolade, opportunity, and professional blessing."

117. "I am a leader, a visionary, and a trailblazer in my profession."

118. "I am constantly surrounded by opportunities to excel, grow, and lead."

119. "Every setback is a setup for a greater professional comeback."

120. *"I am a vital asset to my team, my organization, and my industry."*

121. *"I am inspired to bring innovative ideas and solutions to the table."*

122. *"I am blessed with a career that aligns with my passion and purpose."*

123. *"I am a beacon of positivity, motivation, and inspiration in my workplace."*

124. *"I am ahead of the curve, leading with vision, passion, and purpose."*

125. *"Every day, I make progress towards my professional dreams and goals."*

126. *"I am a magnet for success, abundance, and prosperity in my career."*

127. *"I deserve every professional opportunity, recognition, and blessing."*

128. *"I am a leader, a motivator, and a force to be reckoned with in my field."*

129. *"I am surrounded by opportunities to learn, excel, and succeed."*

130. *"Every challenge is a steppingstone to greater success in my career."*

131. *"I am a vital asset to my organization, my team, and my profession."*

132. *"I am constantly inspired to innovate, create, and lead in my field."*

133. *"I am blessed with a career that brings me joy, success, and fulfillment."*

134. *"I am a beacon of professional positivity, inspiration, and motivation."*

135. *"I am in the right place at the right time for professional growth."*

136. *"I am a magnet for success, prosperity, and growth in my career."*

137. *"I deserve every accolade, promotion, and professional blessing."*

138. *"I am a leader, a visionary, and a game-changer in my profession."*

139. "I am constantly surrounded by opportunities to excel, grow, and lead."

140. "Every setback is a setup for a greater comeback in my career."

141. "I am a vital asset to my team, my organization, and my industry."

142. "I am inspired to bring fresh ideas and innovations to the table."

143. "I am blessed with a career that aligns with my passion and purpose."

144. "I am a beacon of positivity, motivation, and inspiration in my workplace."

145. "I am ahead of the game, leading with vision, purpose, and passion."

146. "Every day, I progress towards my professional goals and dreams."

147. "I am a magnet for success, abundance, and prosperity in my career."

148. "I deserve every professional opportunity, accolade, and blessing."

149. "I am a leader, a motivator, and a force to be reckoned with in my field."

150. "I am surrounded by opportunities to excel and succeed in my career."

Remember, success isn't just about reaching the top; it's about lifting others as you climb. Every challenge is a hidden blessing, every setback a setup for a comeback. With faith, determination, and the right mindset, you can conquer any Goliath. Let's keep winning. You got this. God bless.

Purpose & Direction

"The purpose of life is not to be happy. It is to be useful, honorable, compassionate, and to have it make some difference."
- Ralph Waldo Emerson

"Life is a journey that must be traveled no matter how bad the roads and accommodations."
- Oliver Goldsmith

"Your purpose in life is to find your purpose and give your whole heart and soul to it."
- Buddha

"True happiness... is not attained through self-gratification, but through fidelity to a worthy purpose."
- Helen Keller

"Efforts and courage are not enough without purpose and direction."
- John F. Kennedy

The Compass Within: Navigating Life's True North

In our modern age, filled with distractions and countless paths to choose from, finding one's true purpose and direction can feel overwhelming. But what if we already possess an internal compass, a divine guide rooted in ancient wisdom and biblical principles, waiting to point us towards our true north?

James was a 21st-century man living in a world where trends, social media, and the opinions of others influenced every decision. He felt lost, like a ship adrift at sea, directionless. While cleaning out his grandmother's attic one day, he discovered an old, worn-out compass. Intrigued, he remembered a story she once told him about the Israelites, who, despite wandering in the desert, were guided by a pillar of clouds by day and a pillar of fire by night. They had divine direction, even in their confusion. Feeling inspired, James decided to treat this compass as his spiritual guide. Instead of seeking external validation, he would turn inwards, seeking guidance from that divine spark within, his personal pillar of cloud and fire. With a renewed sense of purpose, James began his mornings with affirmations:

"I am divinely guided in every step I take."

"My purpose is clear, and my path is set before me."

"I trust the journey because I trust the Guide."

"Every challenge is a redirection towards my true north."

"Let's keep winning, for my compass always points to victory."

James began to share his newfound wisdom with friends and family. "*In a world that constantly shouts at you,*" he'd say, "*learn to listen to the whisper of your inner compass. It knows the way.*" He advised them to set aside time daily, away from the noise, to connect with their inner selves, their divine compass. "*You got this,*" he'd assure them, "*because the same God who guided the Israelites is guiding you.*"

As the days turned into weeks and weeks into months, James found himself more aligned with his purpose than ever before. He often reflected on his journey, the missteps, the moments of doubt, and the divine interventions. He realized that every detour, every roadblock, was a lesson, a nudge towards his true direction.

Examples of Negative Self-Talk for "Purpose & Direction"

"I'm lost and directionless."

"I'll never find my true purpose."

"Others seem so sure; why can't I be?"

"Maybe I'm just meant to drift aimlessly."

"I've wasted so much time; it's too late now."

"I'm not special; I don't have a unique purpose."

"I'm scared of choosing the wrong path."

"I don't have what it takes to follow my dreams."

"It's safer just to follow the crowd."

"I'm not wise or intuitive enough to find my way."

Alright, let's dig a little deeper. What negative self-talk have you caught yourself saying or heard others say? This is your chance to confront those limiting beliefs head-on. Jot down your thoughts right here, or flip to the extra pages at the end of the book to really dive in. You got this—let's keep winning and turning those negative thoughts into positive vibes. God bless.

....

....

....

....

....

Reflection Questions

"When have I felt most aligned with my purpose, and what was I doing at that time?"

"What activities or tasks make me lose track of time and feel deeply fulfilled?"

"If I could set aside all fears and doubts, what direction would I choose for my life?"

"How can I daily tune into my inner compass and drown out external noise?"

"What small step can I take today to move closer to my true north?"

Dive into these reflection questions and let your thoughts flow. Whether you jot down your answers right here or flip to the extra pages at the end of the book, make this space your own. You got this—let's keep winning. God bless.

....

....

....

....

....

....

....

....

....

Purpose and Direction

STEPS NO.	STEPS	DESCRIPTION &EXAMPLES
Step 1	Identify Negative Self-Talk or Actions	The first step is to become aware of the negative self-talk or actions that are hindering your sense of purpose and direction. **Example:** "I don't know what I'm doing with my life."
Step 2	Trace the Root Cause	Dig deep to find the root cause of this negative self-talk or action. Is it fear, past experiences, or societal expectations? **Example:** Fear of failure or societal pressure to follow a certain path.
Step 3	Challenge and Reframe	Challenge these negative thoughts or actions by asking if they are based on facts or assumptions. Reframe them into more constructive thoughts. **Example:** "Is it true that I don't know what I'm doing, or am I just afraid to take the next step?"
Step 4	Replace with Positive Affirmations	Replace the negative self-talk with positive affirmations that align with your sense of purpose and direction. **Example:** "I am guided in my journey and every step I take brings me closer to my purpose."
Step 5	Take Action & Build Better Habits	Implement actions that align with your new positive affirmations. Make these actions habitual to solidify your sense of purpose and direction. **Example:** Start a daily journal to track your progress toward your goals.

Positive Affirmations / Self-Talk for "Purpose & Direction"

1. *"Every day, I align more with my true purpose."*

2. *"God has a unique plan for me, and I'm living it."*

3. *"I am guided by a divine compass, leading me to my destiny."*

4. *"Every step I take is a step towards my purpose."*

5. *"I trust the journey, even when I can't see the destination."*

6. *"Let's keep winning by staying true to our calling."*

7. *"The universe conspires to lead me to my true north."*

8. *"Every challenge is a redirection towards my purpose."*

9. *"I am more than my past; I am my potential."*

10. *"God bless my journey and the path I'm on."*

11. *"I am exactly where I need to be."*

12. *"Every day, my purpose becomes clearer."*

13. *"I am a beacon of light, shining with purpose."*

14. *"My direction is more defined with each passing day."*

15. *"I trust the signs that guide me."*

16. *"I am divinely directed and passionately purposeful."*

17. *"The universe has a grand plan for me."*

18. *"Every experience is molding me for my purpose."*

19. *"I am driven, not by success, but by purpose."*

20. *"Let's embrace the journey and the direction it takes us."*

21. *"I am not lost; I am on a divine detour."*

22. *"Every detour leads me closer to my destiny."*

23. *"I am fueled by passion and purpose."*

24. *"God bless every step I take, for it's divinely guided."*

25. *"I am not defined by others; my purpose defines me."*

26. *"Every morning, I wake up with a clearer sense of direction."*

27. *"I am not wandering; I am on a purposeful journey."*

28. *"Let's keep winning by trusting our divine direction."*

29. *"I am led by dreams, driven by purpose."*

30. *"The universe sends signs, and I am attuned to them."*

31. *"I am not waiting for a sign; I am the sign."*

32. *"Every prayer I make guides me closer to my purpose."*

33. *"I am on a mission, divinely assigned and directed."*

34. *"God bless my endeavors, for they align with my purpose."*

35. *"I don't chase success; I chase purpose and direction."*

36. *"Every setback is a setup for a purposeful comeback."*

37. *"I am more than my job; I am my purpose."*

38. *"Let's keep winning by aligning with our divine purpose."*

39. *"I am not aimlessly drifting; I am purposefully directed."*

40. *"Every day, I make choices that align with my direction."*

41. *"I am not confused; I am just recalibrating my direction."*

42. *"God bless my path, for it's unique and purposeful."*

43. *"I am not lost in the crowd; I stand out with purpose."*

44. *"Every dream I chase is a step towards my direction."*

45. *"I am not swayed by the world; I am grounded in my purpose."*

46. *"Let's embrace our unique paths and purpose."*

47. *"I am not defined by society; my purpose defines me."*

48. *"Every challenge is a chance to realign with my direction."*

49. *"I am not aimless; I am purpose-driven."*

50. *"God bless every challenge, for it redirects me to my purpose."*

51. *"I am not wandering; I am exploring my direction."*

52. *"Every person I meet is a signpost to my purpose."*

53. *"I am not waiting for a map; I am creating my path."*

54. *"Let's keep winning by staying true to our direction."*

55. *"I am not swayed by opinions; I am firm in my purpose."*

56. *"Every detour is a divine redirection."*

57. *"I am not chasing fame; I am chasing purpose."*

58. *"God bless my journey, for it's filled with purposeful lessons."*

59. *"I am not lost; I am just finding my true direction."*

60. *"Every decision I make is guided by my purpose."*

61. *"Let's embrace the detours, for they lead to our purpose."*

62. *"I am not swayed by trends; I am grounded in my direction."*

63. *"Every obstacle is an opportunity to find my true purpose."*

64. *"I am not chasing the world; I am chasing my purpose."*

65. *"God bless every step, even the missteps, for they guide me."*

66. *"I am not in a race; I am on a purposeful journey."*

67. *"Every doubt is a chance to reaffirm my direction."*

68. *"I am not defined by failures; I am defined by my purpose."*

69. *"Let's keep winning by trusting our purposeful journey."*

70. *"I am not chasing dreams; I am living my purpose."*

71. *"Every roadblock is a sign to find a new direction."*

72. *"I am not swayed by doubts; I am firm in my purpose."*

73. *"God bless my doubts, for they make my purpose clearer."*

74. *"I am not waiting for a sign; I am living my purpose."*

75. *"Every challenge is a chance to find a new direction."*

76. *"Let's embrace the unknown, for it's filled with purpose."*

77. *"I am not defined by the world; my purpose defines me."*

78. *"Every fear is a chance to realign with my direction."*

79. *"I am not chasing shadows; I am chasing my purpose."*

80. *"God bless every fear, for it makes my direction clearer."*

81. *"I am not in the dark; I am guided by my purposeful light."*

82. *"Every doubt is a detour to my true direction."*

83. *"I am not swayed by the noise; I am tuned into my purpose."*

84. *"Let's keep winning by drowning the doubts with purpose."*

85. *"I am not waiting for validation; I am living my purpose."*

86. *"Every setback is a setup for a purposeful direction."*

87. *"I am not chasing validation; I am grounded in my purpose."*

88. *"God bless every setback, for it's a redirection to my purpose."*

89. *"I am not in a maze; I am on a purposeful path."*

90. *"Every hurdle is a chance to reaffirm my direction."*

91. *"Let's embrace the hurdles, for they guide us to our purpose."*

92. *"I am not chasing wind; I am grounded in my direction."*

93. *"Every tear is a step closer to my purpose."*

94. *"I am not in a storm; I am finding my purposeful direction."*

95. *"God bless every tear, for it clears my path to purpose."*

96. *"I am not in a whirlwind; I am grounded in my direction."*

97. *"Every laugh is a signpost to my purpose."*

98. *"I am not in chaos; I am finding my purposeful calm."*

99. *"Let's keep winning by laughing in the face of doubts."*

100. *"I am not in a rut; I am carving out my direction."*

101. *"Every smile is a step closer to my purpose."*

102. *"I am not in despair; I am rising with purpose."*

103. *"God bless every smile, for it lights up my purposeful path."*

104. *"I am not in a pit; I am climbing in my direction."*

105. *"Every joy is a signpost to my purpose."*

106. *"I am not sinking; I am soaring with purpose."*

107. *"Let's keep winning by finding joy in our direction."*

108. *"I am not in a fog; I am clearing my purposeful path."*

109. *"Every moment is a step closer to my direction."*

110. *"I am not drifting; I am driving with purpose."*

111. *"God bless every moment, for it's filled with purpose."*

112. *"I am not in a daze; I am dazzled by my direction."*

113. *"Every breath is a signpost to my purpose."*

114. *"I am not suffocating; I am breathing with purpose."*

115. *"Let's keep winning by breathing life into our direction."*

116. *"I am not in a bind; I am breaking free with purpose."*

117. *"Every heartbeat is a step closer to my direction."*

118. *"I am not confined; I am expanding with purpose."*

119. *"God bless every heartbeat, for it beats with purpose."*

120. *"I am not in chains; I am charting my direction."*

121. *"Every whisper is a signpost to my purpose."*

122. *"I am not silenced; I am speaking with purpose."*

123. *"Let's keep winning by whispering words of direction."*

124. *"I am not in a cage; I am carving out my purpose."*

125. *"Every shout is a step closer to my direction."*

126. *"I am not muted; I am magnified with purpose."*

127. *"God bless every shout, for it echoes with purpose."*

128. *"I am not in shadows; I am shining with direction."*

129. *"Every step is a signpost to my purpose."*

130. *"I am not faltering; I am firm in my purpose."*

131. *"Let's keep winning by stepping in our direction."*

132. *"I am not in a slump; I am scaling my purposeful peak."*

133. *"Every leap is a step closer to my direction."*

134. *"I am not retreating; I am rising with purpose."*

135. *"God bless every leap, for it leaps with purpose."*

136. *"I am not in a trench; I am trekking in my direction."*

137. *"Every sprint is a signpost to my purpose."*

138. *"I am not crawling; I am cruising with purpose."*

139. *"Let's keep winning by sprinting towards our direction."*

140. *"I am not in a hole; I am helming my purposeful ship."*

141. *"Every dance is a step closer to my direction."*

142. *"I am not stumbling; I am striding with purpose."*

143. *"God bless every dance, for it dances with purpose."*

144. *"I am not in a bind; I am buoyed by my direction."*

145. *"Every song is a signpost to my purpose."*

146. *"I am not sinking; I am singing with purpose."*

147. *"Let's keep winning by singing songs of direction."*

148. *"I am not in a blur; I am beaming with purpose."*

149. *"Every word is a step closer to my direction."*

150. *"I am not mumbling; I am manifesting with purpose. God bless."*

Remember, Purpose and Direction are the compasses of our soul. Life's journey is filled with twists and turns, but we'll always find our way with faith as our compass. Trust in that divine guidance, lean into your purpose, and always remember, you got this. Let's keep winning. God bless.

Resilience & Determination

"Our greatest glory is not in never falling, but in rising every time we fall."
- Confucius

"It's not that I'm so smart, it's just that I stay with problems longer."
- Albert Einstein

"You may have to fight a battle more than once to win it."
- Margaret Thatcher

"Success is not final, failure is not fatal: It is the courage to continue that counts."
- Winston Churchill

"It does not matter how slowly you go as long as you do not stop."
- Confucius

The Unyielding Oak: Standing Tall in Life's Storms

In our modern world, challenges come in many forms, from personal setbacks to global crises. But the true measure of our spirit isn't in the challenges we face but in how we rise after falling. Drawing from biblical wisdom, we find the strength of resilience and determination, akin to the mighty oak that stands tall regardless of the storms it endures.

James was a 21st-century man, living in a world of instant gratifications and fleeting joys. But life wasn't always kind. He lost his job, faced health challenges, and struggled with mounting debts. One evening, feeling defeated, he wandered into a quiet park and found himself under a massive oak tree. Its grandeur and stillness amidst the bustling city intrigued him. He recalled a biblical story his mother narrated about Job, a man who, despite losing everything, never lost his faith. Job's resilience wasn't about never facing hardships but about his unwavering faith and determination to move forward, trusting in a higher plan. Inspired, James saw the oak as a symbol of his journey. Just as the tree had deep roots and stood tall through seasons and storms, he too could anchor himself in faith and face life's challenges with unwavering determination. With a renewed spirit, James began his days with affirmations:

"I am rooted in faith, unyielding to life's storms."

"Challenges are but seasons; my spirit remains eternal and strong."

"With every setback, I rise taller, stronger, and more determined."

"I trust the journey, for I am guided by a divine hand."

"Let's keep winning, for my spirit is indomitable."

James began sharing his story of the oak tree and Job with others. He advised them to find their own symbols of strength, to anchor themselves in times of adversity. "Life will test you," he'd say, "but remember, the deeper the roots, the taller the tree. You got this."

As days turned into months, James found himself not just recovering from his setbacks but thriving. He often sat under the oak, reflecting on his growth, the lessons learned, and the divine guidance that saw him through. He realized true resilience wasn't about avoiding challenges but embracing them, learning from them, and emerging stronger.

Negative Self-Talk for "Resilience & Determination"

"I can't handle this."

"I always give up too easily."

"Why does this always happen to me?"

"I'm not strong enough for this challenge."

"I'll never recover from this setback."

"Others are so much more resilient than me."

"I'm just not cut out for this."

"Every time I try, I fail."

"I'm cursed with bad luck."

"I should just accept that I'm a quitter."

Alright, let's dig a little deeper. What negative self-talk have you caught yourself saying or heard others say? This is your chance to confront those limiting beliefs head-on. Jot down your thoughts right here, or flip to the extra pages at the end of the book to really dive in. You got this—let's keep winning and turning those negative thoughts into positive vibes. God bless.

....

....

....

....

....

Reflection Questions

"What challenges have I overcome in the past that prove my strength and resilience?"

"How can I anchor myself in faith and determination during tough times?"

"What lessons have life's setbacks taught me?"

"How can I turn my adversities into opportunities for growth?"

"Who or what can be my 'oak tree' – a symbol of strength and resilience?"

Dive into these reflection questions and let your thoughts flow. Whether you jot down your answers right here or flip to the extra pages at the end of the book, make this space your own. You got this—let's keep winning. God bless.

....

....

....

....

....

....

....

....

....

....

Resilience and Determination

STEPS NO.	STEPS	DESCRIPTION &EXAMPLES
Step 1	**Identify Negative Self-Talk or Actions**	The first step is to recognize the negative self-talk or actions that are hindering your resilience and determination. **Examples:** "I can't do this," "I'll never succeed," "Why bother trying?"
Step 2	**Trace the Root Cause**	Dig deep to find the root cause of this negative self-talk or action. Understanding the origin can help you address it effectively. **Examples:** Fear of failure, past experiences, societal expectations.
Step 3	**Challenge and Reframe**	Challenge these negative thoughts and reframe them into positive affirmations or constructive actions. **Examples:** "I can learn from this," "Every attempt brings me closer to success," "I am resilient."
Step 4	**Implement Positive Affirmations and Actions**	Actively incorporate these positive affirmations into your daily routine and take actions that align with them. **Examples:** Daily affirmations, setting achievable goals, seeking support.
Step 5	**Evaluate and Adjust**	Periodically evaluate your progress. Are the new affirmations and actions helping you become more resilient and determined? If not, adjust your approach. **Examples:** Weekly check-ins, tracking milestones, celebrating small wins.

Positive Affirmations / Self-Talk for "Resilience & Determination"

1. *"Every challenge I face is an opportunity for growth. Let's keep winning!"*

2. *"I am stronger than any obstacle in my path."*

3. *"With every setback, my comeback is even more powerful."*

4. *"I've faced tough times and emerged victorious. This is no different."*

5. *"God gives the hardest battles to his strongest soldiers. I'm ready."*

6. *"I am resilient, determined, and unstoppable."*

7. *"Every 'no' I hear pushes me closer to a 'yes'."*

8. *"I've got the spirit of a warrior. I won't back down."*

9. *"Challenges shape me, but they will never define me."*

10. *"I am the captain of my fate, the master of my soul."*

11. *"With God by my side, I can weather any storm."*

12. *"Every day, I grow stronger and more determined."*

13. *"I am built from my hardships, and they make me resilient."*

14. *"I've got this. No matter what comes my way."*

15. *"Setbacks are just setups for greater comebacks."*

16. *"I am more than my struggles. I am my victories."*

17. *"Every challenge is a lesson. I'm learning and growing."*

18. *"I am determined to succeed, no matter how long it takes."*

19. *"My spirit is unbreakable. My will is unshakeable."*

20. *"I've been down before, but I always rise. Always."*

21. *"I am a force to be reckoned with. Challenges, beware!"*

22. *"With faith and determination, I can move mountains."*

23. *"I am destined for greatness, and no obstacle can deter me."*

24. *"Every time I fall, I rise higher than before."*

25. *"I am resilient, for I've been molded by my challenges."*

26. *"I've got the heart of a lion. I won't give up."*

27. *"God bless my journey, for it's making me who I am."*

28. *"I am determined to shine, even in the midst of storms."*

29. *"I am a warrior, not a worrier."*

30. *"Every challenge I conquer adds to my success story."*

31. *"I am built to withstand, to endure, and to thrive."*

32. *"I've got the strength of my past and the hope of my future."*

33. *"I am unstoppable because I continue despite my failures."*

34. *"Let's keep winning, for every trial only adds to our triumphs."*

35. *"I am a beacon of resilience and determination."*

36. *"Every scar I have is a testament to my resilience."*

37. *"I am determined to turn every stumbling block into a stepping stone."*

38. *"I've got this. Today, tomorrow, always."*

39. *"I am the embodiment of perseverance and grit."*

40. *"God's got my back, and with Him, I can face anything."*

41. *"I am relentless in my pursuit of my dreams."*

42. *"I am a testament to the power of determination."*

43. *"I am built to last, to endure, and to overcome."*

44. "Every challenge is just another chapter in my success story."

45. "I am the master of my destiny, the author of my story."

46. "With unwavering determination, I chase my dreams."

47. "I am resilient, for life has taught me to be."

48. "I've got the spirit of a champion. I won't be defeated."

49. "I am determined to rise, no matter how many times I fall."

50. "God bless my journey, for every twist and turn only makes me stronger."

51. "I am a powerhouse of resilience and determination."

52. "I've got the will to win and the heart to endure."

53. "I am unstoppable in my pursuit of excellence."

54. "I am resilient, for I've faced the storms and still stand tall."

55. "I am determined to be the best version of myself."

56. "I've got this, for I am made of strength and courage."

57. "I am a force of nature, unyielding and unbreakable."

58. "Every challenge I face only adds to my legacy of success."

59. "I am the epitome of grit and grace."

60. "With God by my side, every challenge becomes an opportunity."

61. "I am relentless, for I know my worth."

62. "I am resilient, for I've been tested and have triumphed."

63. "I've got the heart of a fighter and the spirit of a winner."

64. "I am determined to leave a mark, to make a difference."

65. "God bless my spirit, for it's unbreakable."

66. *"I am a beacon of hope, strength, and determination."*

67. *"I've got this, for my spirit is indomitable."*

68. *"I am the embodiment of resilience in the face of adversity."*

69. *"I am determined to succeed, for I've seen the power of perseverance."*

70. *"I am a warrior, forged in the fires of challenges."*

71. *"I've got the spirit of resilience, and I won't be broken."*

72. *"I am a testament to the power of determination and faith."*

73. *"I've got this, for I am more than my challenges."*

74. *"I am the face of resilience, determination, and grit."*

75. *"God bless my journey, for every challenge only makes me more resilient."*

76. *"I am unstoppable, for I am fueled by determination."*

77. *"I've got the heart of a lion, and I won't be deterred."*

78. *"I am resilient, for I've faced the odds and emerged victorious."*

79. *"I am determined to shine, even when faced with challenges."*

80. *"I've got this, for my spirit is unyielding."*

81. *"I am the embodiment of resilience in the 21st century."*

82. *"I am determined to rise, for I've seen the power of faith."*

83. *"I've got the spirit of a champion, and I won't back down."*

84. *"I am a beacon of hope in the face of adversity."*

85. *"God bless my spirit, for it's filled with determination."*

86. *"I am relentless in my pursuit of my dreams."*

87. *"I've got this, for I am made of resilience and grit."*

88. *"I am a testament to the power of determination in the modern age."*

89. *"I am resilient, for I've been molded by my challenges."*

90. *"I've got the heart of a warrior, and I won't be defeated."*

91. *"I am determined to make a difference, to leave a legacy."*

92. *"God bless my journey, for it's filled with resilience and hope."*

93. *"I am unstoppable, for I am driven by determination."*

94. *"I've got this, for I am more than my setbacks."*

95. *"I am the face of modern-day resilience and determination."*

96. *"I am relentless, for I've seen the power of perseverance."*

97. *"I've got the spirit of a winner, and I won't be broken."*

98. *"I am a beacon of determination in a world of challenges."*

99. *"God bless my spirit, for it's unbreakable and determined."*

100. *"I am unstoppable, for I am fueled by resilience."*

101. *"I've got this, for my spirit is indomitable."*

102. *"I am the embodiment of modern-day determination."*

103. *"I am resilient, for I've faced the odds and still stand tall."*

104. *"I am determined to shine, for I've seen the power of faith."*

105. *"I've got the heart of a champion, and I won't be deterred."*

106. *"I am a beacon of hope, resilience, and determination."*

107. *"God bless my journey, for every setback only makes me stronger."*

108. *"I am unstoppable, for I am driven by grit and grace."*

109. *"I've got this, for I am more than my challenges."*

110. *"I am the face of resilience in the 21st century."*

111. "I am determined to rise, for I've seen the power of hope."

112. "I've got the spirit of a fighter, and I won't back down."

113. "I am a beacon of determination in a world of setbacks."

114. "God bless my spirit, for it's filled with hope and resilience."

115. "I am relentless in my pursuit of excellence."

116. "I've got this, for I am made of determination and faith."

117. "I am the embodiment of resilience in the modern age."

118. "I am determined to shine, even in the face of adversity."

119. "I've got the heart of a lion, and I won't be broken."

120. "I am a beacon of hope and determination in a challenging world."

121. "God bless my journey, for it's filled with resilience and determination."

122. "I am unstoppable, for I am driven by hope and grit."

123. "I've got this, for my spirit is unyielding and determined."

124. "I am the face of modern-day determination and resilience."

125. "I am relentless, for I've seen the power of hope and faith."

126. "I've got the spirit of a winner, and I won't be deterred."

127. "I am a beacon of resilience in a world of challenges."

128. "God bless my spirit, for it's filled with determination and hope."

129. "I am unstoppable, for I am driven by resilience and faith."

130. "I've got this, for I am more than my setbacks and challenges."

131. "I am the embodiment of modern-day hope and determination."

132. "I am resilient, for I've faced the odds and emerged victorious."

133. "I am determined to shine, for I've seen the power of resilience."

134. "I've got the heart of a champion, and I won't be broken."

135. "I am a beacon of determination and hope in a challenging world."

136. "God bless my journey, for every setback only makes me more determined."

137. "I am unstoppable, for I am driven by hope and determination."

138. "I've got this, for my spirit is filled with resilience and hope."

139. "I am the face of resilience and determination in the 21st century."

140. "I am relentless, for I've seen the power of hope and determination."

141. "I've got the spirit of a winner, and I won't be deterred."

142. "I am a beacon of hope and resilience in a world of challenges."

143. "God bless my spirit, for it's unbreakable and determined."

144. "I am unstoppable, for I am driven by resilience and hope."

145. "I've got this, for I am more than my setbacks and challenges."

146. "I am the embodiment of hope and determination in the modern age."

147. "I am resilient, for I've faced the odds and still stand tall."

148. "I am determined to shine, even in the face of adversity."

149. "I've got the heart of a lion, and I won't be defeated."

150. "I am a beacon of determination and resilience, ready to face any challenge. Let's keep winning!"

Remember, Life's journey is filled with challenges, but with resilience and determination, we can conquer anything. Life's storms are inevitable, but so is our inner strength. Trust the journey, embrace the challenges, and always know you got this. Let's keep winning. God bless."

Self-Esteem & Confidence

"To love oneself is the beginning of a lifelong romance."
- Oscar Wilde

"Believe in yourself and all that you are. Know that there is something inside you that is greater than any obstacle."
- Christian D. Larson

"You yourself, as much as anybody in the entire universe, deserve your love and affection."
- Buddha

"Low self-esteem is like driving through life with your handbrake on."
- Maxwell Maltz

"To be yourself in a world that is constantly trying to make you something else is the greatest accomplishment."
- Ralph Waldo Emerson

The Mirror of Truth: Seeing Beyond the Reflection

In today's fast-paced, digital-driven 21st century, the mirror we often look into isn't just made of glass. It's the mirror of social media, the opinions of others, and the unrealistic standards set by society. But what if we could see beyond that reflection? What if we could tap into an age-old wisdom, a biblical principle, that reminds us of our inherent worth and divine purpose?

Sarah was a modern woman living in a bustling city, juggling her job, social life, and the constant barrage of social media notifications. Every day, she would scroll through her feed, seeing her friends' achievements, their vacations, and their seemingly perfect lives. It made her feel inadequate like she was lagging behind in this race of life. One day, while cleaning her attic, she stumbled upon an old, dusty mirror. As she wiped it clean, she noticed it wasn't reflecting her current self but a radiant version of her. Confused, she recalled a story her grandmother used to tell her about the biblical tale of Moses. Despite his initial self-doubt and lack of confidence, Moses was chosen by God to lead because he had a heart willing to serve. He wasn't defined by the opinions of others but by his divine purpose. Inspired, Sarah decided to treat this mirror as her "Mirror of Truth." Every morning, instead of diving into the digital world, she would look into this mirror, reminding herself of her divine worth, her unique journey, and her purpose. With newfound inspiration, Sarah penned down affirmations that she would recite every day:

"I am chosen, loved, and crafted with a divine purpose."

"The opinions of others do not define me; my Creator does."

"Every challenge is an opportunity for growth, handpicked for me."

"I am more than my mistakes; I am my potential."

"Let's keep winning, for every step I take is ordained and blessed."

Sarah began to share her story with her friends. She advised them to find their own "Mirror of Truth," a space or moment where they disconnect from the world's noise and connect with their true selves. "*Remember*," she would say, "*comparison is the thief of joy. Your journey is uniquely yours. Embrace it, flaws and all. You got this.*"

Months passed, and Sarah's perspective shifted. She felt more grounded, confident, and at peace. Every now and then, she would sit in silence, reflecting on her growth, her challenges, and the divine guidance that saw her through. And as she did, she felt a deep connection with the biblical heroes, ordinary people with extraordinary faith who trusted in a power greater than themselves.

Examples of Negative Self-Talk for "Self-Esteem & Confidence"

"I'm not good enough."

"Why can't I be more like them?"

"I always mess things up."

"No one truly cares about me."

"I'm a failure."

"I'll never achieve my dreams."

"I don't deserve happiness."

"I'm not smart or talented."

"People will judge me."

"I'm just not cut out for this."

Alright, let's dig a little deeper. What negative self-talk have you caught yourself saying or heard others say? This is your chance to confront those limiting beliefs head-on. Jot down your thoughts right here, or flip to the extra pages at the end of the book to really dive in. You got this—let's keep winning and turning those negative thoughts into positive vibes. God bless.

....

....

....

....

Reflection Questions

"When was the last time I truly felt proud of myself, and why?"

"What qualities do I possess that I genuinely love and appreciate?"

"How does comparing myself to others serve me, and how does it hinder me?"

"What is one step I can take today to affirm my worth and boost my confidence?"

"How can I create a daily ritual that reminds me of my divine purpose and inherent value?"

Dive into these reflection questions and let your thoughts flow. Whether you jot down your answers right here or flip to the extra pages at the end of the book, make this space your own. You got this—let's keep winning. God bless.

....

....

....

....

....

....

....

....

....

Self-Esteem and Confidence

STEPS NO.	STEPS	DESCRIPTION &EXAMPLES
Step 1	Identify Negative Self-Talk or Actions	Recognize the negative self-talk or actions that are hindering your self-esteem and confidence.
Step 2	Trace the Root Cause	Dig deep to find the underlying cause or belief that triggers this negative self-talk or action.
Step 3	Challenge and Reframe	Challenge these negative thoughts or actions by asking questions like, "Is this really true?" or "What evidence do I have for this belief?" Then, reframe them into positive affirmations.
Step 4	Implement Positive Affirmations	Consistently use your new positive affirmations to replace the old negative self-talk. Use them especially in situations where you'd typically resort to negativity.
Step 5	Develop and Reinforce Better Habits	As you practice these affirmations, start taking actions that align with them. Monitor your progress and adjust as needed.

Positive Affirmations / Self-Talk for "Self-Esteem & Confidence"

1. *"I am worthy of all the good life has to offer."*

2. *"Every challenge I face is an opportunity to grow."*

3. *"I deserve love, success, and happiness."*

4. *"God has a plan for me, and it's filled with blessings."*

5. *"I am stronger than any obstacle in my path."*

6. *"Every day, I'm becoming a better version of myself."*

7. *"I trust in my journey and God's plan for me."*

8. *"I am capable of achieving my dreams."*

9. *"My potential is limitless."*

10. *"I deserve every compliment I receive."*

11. *"I am not my mistakes; I am my potential."*

12. *"Every setback is a setup for a comeback. Let's keep winning!"*

13. *"I am a beacon of love and confidence."*

14. *"I believe in myself and my abilities."*

15. *"I am surrounded by love, and everything is possible."*

16. *"I am a masterpiece, handcrafted by the Divine."*

17. *"I am enough, always have been, always will be."*

18. *"I am resilient, strong, and brave."*

19. *"I deserve every opportunity that comes my way."*

20. *"I am a magnet for success and good vibes."*

21. *"I am a winner, even before the victory is visible."*

22. *"I am loved, cherished, and valued."*

23. *"I am constantly evolving and improving."*

24. *"I am the architect of my life; I build its foundation and choose its content."*

25. *"I am blessed with talents and skills that bring value to the world."*

26. *"I am a force to be reckoned with."*

27. *"I am in control of my thoughts, feelings, and actions."*

28. *"I am on a journey, and every step is shaping me."*

29. *"I am not defined by my past but inspired by my future."*

30. *"I am a beacon of hope and inspiration for others."*

31. *"I deserve respect and kindness."*

32. *"I am a warrior, not a worrier."*

33. *"I am more than my doubts and fears."*

34. *"I am guided by faith, not driven by fear."*

35. *"I am constantly surrounded by opportunities to grow and thrive."*

36. *"I am a positive force, and my spirit is unbreakable."*

37. *"I am in charge of how I feel, and today I choose happiness."*

38. *"I am destined for greatness."*

39. *"I am a magnet for miracles."*

40. *"I am a living testament to what's possible with faith and determination."*

41. *"I am proud of who I am and who I'm becoming."*

42. *"I am walking my own path at my own pace."*

43. *"I am the captain of my ship and the master of my fate."*

44. *"I deserve every dream I chase."*

45. *"I am filled with endless potential."*

46. *"I am not here to be average; I'm here to be awesome."*

47. *"I am a diamond, unbreakable and valuable."*

48. *"I am constantly in awe of what I'm capable of."*

49. *"I am a blessing to the world."*

50. *"I am loved beyond measure."*

51. *"I am not defined by others' opinions but by my truth and spirit."*

52. *"I am a powerhouse; I am indestructible."*

53. *"I am on a mission, and nothing can stop me."*

54. *"I am a beautiful blend of strength and grace."*

55. *"I am a living, breathing miracle."*

56. *"I am a testament to perseverance and faith."*

57. *"I am the author of my story."*

58. *"I am overflowing with creativity and innovation."*

59. *"I am a beacon of positivity and hope."*

60. *"I am unstoppable in my pursuit of success."*

61. *"I am a magnet for abundance and blessings."*

62. *"I deserve every bit of happiness that comes my way."*

63. *"I am constantly inspired by life's wonders."*

64. *"I am a force of nature, unstoppable in my pursuits."*

65. *"I am cherished, respected, and admired."*

66. *"I am constantly growing, learning, and evolving."*

67. *"I am a masterpiece in progress."*

68. *"I am a magnet for love, success, and prosperity."*

69. *"I deserve all the universe has to offer."*

70. *"I am a shining star, brightening every space I enter."*

71. *"I am a champion, always rising to the challenge."*

72. *"I am a beacon of light in a sometimes-dark world."*

73. *"I am a vessel of love, joy, and peace."*

74. *"I am a trailblazer, forging my own path."*

75. *"I am a dreamer and a doer."*

76. *"I am blessed with a spirit of resilience."*

77. *"I am a magnet for positive experiences."*

78. *"I am a living embodiment of love and light."*

79. *"I am a conqueror, overcoming every challenge."*

80. *"I am a radiant being, full of light and love."*

81. *"I am a visionary, always seeing the bigger picture."*

82. *"I am a leader, guiding others with love and integrity."*

83. *"I am a beacon of hope for those who seek inspiration."*

84. *"I am a warrior of light, always standing in my truth."*

85. *"I am a vessel of endless possibilities."*

86. *"I am a force of nature, always moving forward."*

87. *"I am a beacon of wisdom and insight."*

88. *"I am a magnet for joy, love, and abundance."*

89. *"I am a living testament to the power of faith and determination."*

90. *"I am a beacon of strength and courage."*

91. *"I am a vessel of divine love and light."*

92. *"I am a magnet for blessings and miracles."*

93. *"I am a beacon of positivity and hope."*

94. *"I am a force to be reckoned with."*

95. *"I am a magnet for success and prosperity."*

96. *"I am a beacon of love, light, and wisdom."*

97. *"I am a vessel of endless potential and possibilities."*

98. *"I am a force of nature, unstoppable in my pursuits."*

99. *"I am a beacon of hope, love, and light."*

100. *"I am a magnet for blessings, love, and abundance."*

101. *"I am a beacon of strength, courage, and resilience."*

102. *"I am a vessel of divine wisdom and insight."*

103. *"I am a force to be reckoned with, always standing in my truth."*

104. *"I am a beacon of love, joy, and peace."*

105. *"I am a magnet for success, prosperity, and abundance."*

106. *"I am a beacon of hope, inspiration, and light."*

107. *"I am a vessel of endless love, joy, and peace."*

108. *"I am a force of nature, always moving forward with grace."*

109. *"I am a beacon of wisdom, insight, and love."*

110. *"I am a magnet for blessings, miracles, and love."*

111. *"I am a beacon of strength, resilience, and courage."*

112. *"I am a vessel of divine love, light, and wisdom."*

113. *"I am a force to be reckoned with, always standing in my power."*

114. *"I am a beacon of hope, love, and inspiration."*

115. *"I am a magnet for success, prosperity, and blessings."*

116. *"I am a beacon of light, wisdom, and love."*

117. *"I am a vessel of endless potential and possibilities."*

118. *"I am a force of nature, unstoppable in my pursuits."*

119. *"I am a beacon of love, joy, and peace."*

120. *"I am a magnet for blessings, love, and abundance."*

121. *"I am a beacon of strength, courage, and resilience."*

122. *"I am a vessel of divine wisdom and insight."*

123. *"I am a force to be reckoned with, always standing in my truth."*

124. *"I am a beacon of love, light, and wisdom."*

125. *"I am a magnet for success, prosperity, and abundance."*

126. *"I am a beacon of hope, love, and light."*

127. *"I am a vessel of endless love, joy, and peace."*

128. *"I am a force of nature, always moving forward with grace."*

129. *"I am a beacon of wisdom, insight, and love."*

130. *"I am a magnet for blessings, miracles, and love."*

131. *"I am a beacon of strength, resilience, and courage."*

132. *"I am a vessel of divine love, light, and wisdom."*

133. *"I am a force to be reckoned with, always standing in my power."*

134. *"I am a beacon of hope, love, and inspiration."*

135. *"I am a magnet for success, prosperity, and blessings."*

136. *"I am a beacon of light, wisdom, and love."*

137. *"I am a vessel of endless potential and possibilities."*

138. *"I am a force of nature, unstoppable in my pursuits."*

139. *"I am a beacon of love, joy, and peace."*

140. *"I am a magnet for blessings, love, and abundance."*

141. *"I am a beacon of strength, courage, and resilience."*

142. *"I am a vessel of divine wisdom and insight."*

143. *"I am a force to be reckoned with, always standing in my truth."*

144. *"I am a beacon of love, light, and wisdom."*

145. *"I am a magnet for success, prosperity, and abundance."*

146. *"I am a beacon of hope, love, and light."*

147. *"I am a vessel of endless love, joy, and peace."*

148. *"I am a force of nature, always moving forward with grace."*

149. *"I am a beacon of wisdom, insight, and love."*

150. *"I am a magnet for blessings, miracles, and love."*

Remember, Affirmations are the seeds we plant in the garden of our minds. Water them daily with faith and watch your confidence bloom. Life is a journey, not a race. Embrace your path, trust your divine purpose, and always know you got this. Let's keep winning. God bless.

Self-Improvement & Growth

"There is nothing noble in being superior to your fellow man; true nobility is being superior to your former self."
- Ernest Hemingway

"The only person you should try to be better than is the person you were yesterday."
- Anonymous

"Growth and comfort do not coexist."
- Ginni Rometty

"He who stops being better stops being good."
- Oliver Cromwell

"The best investment you can make is in yourself."
- Warren Buffett

The Garden of Growth: Cultivating Your Divine Potential

In the vast landscape of the 21st century, where change is the only constant, the quest for self-improvement and growth has never been more crucial. Just as a gardener tends to his plants, ensuring they receive adequate sunlight, water, and care, we must nurture our souls, drawing inspiration from biblical principles that have withstood the test of time.

James was a tech-savvy millennial, always on the hunt for the next big app or digital trend. But amidst the digital chaos, he felt an emptiness, a yearning for something more profound. One day, while reading the Bible, he stumbled upon the Parable of the Sower. The story, simple yet profound, spoke of different types of soils and how seeds fared in each. Inspired, James decided to start a physical garden in his backyard. As he began to till the soil, plant seeds, and watch them grow, he realized the garden was a metaphor for his life. The weeds represented his doubts, the rocky soil his challenges, and the fertile ground his potential. As days turned into weeks, James found solace in his garden. He began to recite daily affirmations:

"I am fertile soil, ready to nurture and grow."

"Every challenge, like a seed, holds the potential for growth."

"I am rooted in faith, reaching for the sunlight of my dreams."

"Let's keep winning, for every weed I pull makes room for blossoms."

"With patience and care, I will flourish."

James began to share his gardening journey with friends and family. He'd often say, "*Just as we water plants, we must hydrate our souls with positive thoughts. And as we prune a plant, we must also trim away negative influences.*" His advice was simple: Dedicate time for self-reflection, embrace challenges as growth opportunities, and always, always stay rooted in faith.

As seasons changed, so did James. The garden, once barren, was now a haven of greenery, flowers, and life. James, too, had transformed from a man seeking purpose to one living it. He'd often sit in his garden, reflecting on his journey, drawing parallels between the biblical tales and his life, realizing that personal and spiritual growth was a continuous journey.

Examples of Negative Self-Talk for "Self-Improvement & Growth"

"I'll never change."

"I'm stuck in my ways."

"Others are better than me."

"I don't have what it takes."

"It's too late for me."

"I'm not worthy of success."

"I always fall short."

"Why even try?"

"I'm just not talented."

"I'll never understand."

Alright, let's dig a little deeper. What negative self-talk have you caught yourself saying or heard others say? This is your chance to confront those limiting beliefs head-on. Jot down your thoughts right here, or flip to the extra pages at the end of the book to really dive in. You got this—let's keep winning and turning those negative thoughts into positive vibes. God bless.

....

....

....

....

Reflection Questions

"What 'seeds' am I planting in my life today that will bear fruit tomorrow?"

"Which 'weeds' or negative influences do I need to remove from my life?"

"How can I ensure I'm providing the right 'nutrients' for my personal growth?"

"What lessons from my past can guide my growth journey?"

"How can I stay rooted in faith, even when faced with challenges?"

Dive into these reflection questions and let your thoughts flow. Whether you jot down your answers right here or flip to the extra pages at the end of the book, make this space your own. You got this—let's keep winning. God bless.

....

....

....

....

....

....

....

....

....

....

Self-Improvement and Growth

STEPS NO.	STEPS	DESCRIPTION &EXAMPLES
Step 1	**Identify Negative Self-Talk or Actions**	Recognize the negative self-talk or actions that are holding you back from achieving your goals in self-improvement and growth.
Step 2	**Trace the Root Cause**	Dig deep to find the root cause of this negative self-talk or actions. Is it fear, past experiences, or external influences?
Step 3	**Challenge and Reframe**	Challenge these negative thoughts or actions by asking yourself if they are based on facts or assumptions. Reframe them into positive affirmations.
Step 4	**Implement Positive Affirmations**	Start incorporating these positive affirmations into your daily routine. Take actions that align with your new positive mindset.
Step 5	**Develop and Reinforce Better Habits**	Keep track of your progress. Are your new affirmations and actions leading to better habits and growth? If not, adjust and refine.

Positive Affirmations / Self-Talk for "Self-Improvement & Growth"

1. *"Every day, I'm becoming a better version of myself. Let's keep winning!"*

2. *"I embrace challenges as opportunities for growth. God's got my back."*

3. *"I am constantly evolving and improving. You got this!"*

4. *"Every experience is a lesson, shaping my future."*

5. *"I am worthy of all the growth coming my way."*

6. *"With each sunrise, I find new ways to improve myself."*

7. *"I am committed to learning and growing every single day."*

8. *"Mistakes are stepping stones, leading me to greatness."*

9. *"I am open to new ideas and experiences that foster my growth."*

10. *"Every setback is a setup for a greater comeback. Let's keep winning!"*

11. *"I am in control of my growth and my journey."*

12. *"I embrace change because it leads to self-improvement."*

13. *"I am constantly expanding my horizons and pushing my boundaries."*

14. *"Every day, I strive to be better than I was yesterday."*

15. *"I am a work in progress, and that's okay."*

16. *"I am dedicated to personal growth and self-improvement."*

17. *"I trust the journey and embrace the lessons."*

18. *"I am resilient, always bouncing back stronger."*

19. *"I am open to feedback because it helps me grow."*

20. *"I am a lifelong learner, always seeking knowledge."*

21. "I am committed to my growth journey. God bless my path."

22. "I am constantly outdoing my past self."

23. "I deserve all the growth and opportunities coming my way."

24. "I am adaptable, always evolving with the times."

25. "I am focused on my goals and personal growth."

26. "I am always in a state of growth and expansion."

27. "I am proactive in seeking ways to improve myself."

28. "I am not afraid of change; it's a sign of growth."

29. "I am always ready to learn and grow."

30. "I am empowered by my growth journey."

31. "I am in charge of my destiny and growth."

32. "I am constantly inspired to grow and improve."

33. "I am always looking for ways to better myself."

34. "I am a magnet for growth opportunities."

35. "I am always open to new experiences that foster growth."

36. "I am a student of life, always learning."

37. "I am committed to my self-improvement journey."

38. "I am always pushing my boundaries and expanding my horizons."

39. "I am proud of how far I've come and excited for where I'm going."

40. "I am always seeking knowledge and wisdom."

41. "I am a powerhouse of growth and self-improvement."

42. "I am always in a state of self-reflection and growth."

43. "I am dedicated to becoming the best version of myself."

44. *"I am always finding new ways to challenge myself and grow."*

45. *"I am constantly evolving, and that's my superpower."*

46. *"I am committed to my personal growth journey, no matter the obstacles."*

47. *"I am always finding joy in the journey of self-improvement."*

48. *"I am always pushing myself to new heights."*

49. *"I am a beacon of growth and self-improvement."*

50. *"I am always seeking new experiences that challenge and grow me."*

51. *"I am constantly inspired by my growth journey."*

52. *"I am always looking for ways to better myself and my surroundings."*

53. *"I am a force of nature, always growing and evolving."*

54. *"I am dedicated to my personal and professional growth."*

55. *"I am always finding new ways to improve and evolve."*

56. *"I am a testament to growth and resilience."*

57. *"I am always seeking knowledge and experiences that foster growth."*

58. *"I am a magnet for growth and self-improvement opportunities."*

59. *"I am always pushing my limits and growing in the process."*

60. *"I am a beacon of growth, always shining and evolving."*

61. *"I am committed to my growth journey, no matter the challenges."*

62. *"I am always finding joy in the process of self-improvement."*

63. *"I am a powerhouse of growth and evolution."*

64. *"I am always in a state of self-reflection and improvement."*

65. *"I am dedicated to becoming the best version of myself every day."*

66. *"I am always seeking new challenges that foster growth."*

67. *"I am a testament to the power of growth and resilience."*

68. *"I am always looking for ways to improve and challenge myself."*

69. *"I am a force to be reckoned with, always growing and improving."*

70. *"I am dedicated to my personal and professional growth journey."*

71. *"I am always finding new ways to evolve and improve."*

72. *"I am a beacon of growth, always shining and evolving."*

73. *"I am committed to my growth journey, embracing every challenge."*

74. *"I am always finding joy in the journey of self-improvement."*

75. *"I am a powerhouse of growth and self-improvement."*

76. *"I am always in a state of growth and evolution."*

77. *"I am dedicated to becoming the best version of myself every single day."*

78. *"I am always seeking new experiences that foster growth."*

79. *"I am a testament to the power of growth and evolution."*

80. *"I am always looking for ways to challenge and improve myself."*

81. *"I am a force of nature, always growing and evolving."*

82. *"I am dedicated to my growth journey, no matter the obstacles."*

83. *"I am always finding new ways to improve and evolve."*

84. *"I am a beacon of growth, always shining and evolving."*

85. *"I am committed to my growth journey, no matter the challenges."*

86. *"I am always finding joy in the process of self-improvement."*

87. *"I am a powerhouse of growth and evolution."*

88. *"I am always in a state of self-reflection and growth."*

89. "I am dedicated to becoming the best version of myself every day."

90. "I am always seeking new challenges that foster growth."

91. "I am a testament to the power of growth and resilience."

92. "I am always looking for ways to improve and challenge myself."

93. "I am a force to be reckoned with, always growing and improving."

94. "I am dedicated to my personal and professional growth journey."

95. "I am always finding new ways to evolve and improve."

96. "I am a beacon of growth, always shining and evolving."

97. "I am committed to my growth journey, embracing every challenge."

98. "I am always finding joy in the journey of self-improvement."

99. "I am a powerhouse of growth and self-improvement."

100. "I am always in a state of growth and evolution."

101. "Every day, I'm one step closer to my best self. Let's keep winning!"

102. "I am open to growth in all areas of my life."

103. "I am constantly learning, evolving, and improving."

104. "I am committed to my journey of self-improvement."

105. "I am always seeking knowledge and wisdom to grow."

106. "I am a force of nature, always evolving and growing."

107. "I am dedicated to my growth and self-improvement journey."

108. "I am always pushing my boundaries and expanding my horizons."

109. "I am a beacon of growth and self-improvement."

110. "I am always seeking new experiences that foster growth."

111. "I am a testament to the power of growth and self-improvement."

112. *"I am always looking for ways to challenge and improve myself."*

113. *"I am a force to be reckoned with, always growing and evolving."*

114. *"I am dedicated to my growth journey, no matter the obstacles."*

115. *"I am always finding new ways to improve and evolve."*

116. *"I am a beacon of growth, always shining and evolving."*

117. *"I am committed to my growth journey, no matter the challenges."*

118. *"I am always finding joy in the journey of self-improvement."*

119. *"I am a powerhouse of growth and evolution."*

120. *"I am always in a state of self-reflection and growth."*

121. *"I am dedicated to becoming the best version of myself every day."*

122. *"I am always seeking new challenges that foster growth."*

123. *"I am a testament to the power of growth and resilience."*

124. *"I am always looking for ways to improve and challenge myself."*

125. *"I am a force of nature, always growing and evolving."*

126. *"I am dedicated to my growth journey, no matter the obstacles."*

127. *"I am always finding new ways to improve and evolve."*

128. *"I am a beacon of growth, always shining and evolving."*

129. *"I am committed to my growth journey, embracing every challenge."*

130. *"I am always finding joy in the journey of self-improvement."*

131. *"I am a powerhouse of growth and self-improvement."*

132. *"I am always in a state of growth and evolution."*

133. *"I am dedicated to becoming the best version of myself every single day."*

134. "I am always seeking new experiences that foster growth."

135. "I am a testament to the power of growth and evolution."

136. "I am always looking for ways to challenge and improve myself."

137. "I am a force to be reckoned with, always growing and improving."

138. "I am dedicated to my personal and professional growth journey."

139. "I am always finding new ways to evolve and improve."

140. "I am a beacon of growth, always shining and evolving."

141. "I am committed to my growth journey, no matter the challenges."

142. "I am always finding joy in the process of self-improvement."

143. "I am a powerhouse of growth and evolution."

144. "I am always in a state of self-reflection and growth."

145. "I am dedicated to becoming the best version of myself every day."

146. "I am always seeking new challenges that foster growth."

147. "I am a testament to the power of growth and resilience."

148. "I am always looking for ways to improve and challenge myself."

149. "I am a force of nature, always growing and evolving."

150. "With God's grace, every day I am growing, learning, and improving. Let's keep winning!"

Remember, Growth is a journey, not a destination. Embrace every step, every challenge, and every lesson. Life is a garden, and we are both the gardener and the plant. It's up to us to decide how we grow. Let's keep winning, nurture your soul, and always remember you got this. God bless.

Service & Philanthropy

"The best way to find yourself is to lose yourself in the service of others."
- Mahatma Gandhi

"We make a living by what we get, but we make a life by what we give."
- Winston Churchill

"Service to others is the rent you pay for your room here on Earth."
- Muhammad Ali

"To know even one life has breathed easier because you have lived; that is to have succeeded."
- Ralph Waldo Emerson

"Philanthropy is not about money, it's about feeling the pain of others and caring enough about their needs to help."
- Timothy Pina

The Modern-Day Good Samaritan: Serving Beyond Self

In a world driven by personal gains and self-centered pursuits, the age-old biblical principle of serving others often takes a backseat. But what if, in this 21st-century hustle, we rediscover the joy of giving, the fulfillment in serving, and the blessings of philanthropy?

Meet Jake, a successful entrepreneur in the heart of New York City. With skyscrapers touching the heavens and his business booming, Jake felt on top of the world. Yet, amidst the glitz and glamour, there was a void, an emptiness his wealth couldn't fill. One winter evening, as Jake walked the shimmering streets, he came across an old man, shivering, with a sign that read, *"Anything helps. God bless."* Reminded of the biblical story of the Good Samaritan, Jake felt a tug at his heart. Instead of walking by, he sat beside the man, offering him a warm meal and a listening ear. The old man, Samuel, shared tales of his youth, his dreams, and the series of unfortunate events that led him to the streets. Jake realized that beneath the ragged clothes and weathered skin was a soul, just like his, seeking love, warmth, and understanding. Moved by this encounter, Jake began his mornings with affirmations:

"Today, I choose to serve beyond self."

"In giving, I receive manifold blessings."

"Every soul I meet is a reflection of the Divine."

"Let's keep winning by lifting others."

"Through service, I find my true purpose."

Jake's perspective on life and success transformed. He started a foundation aiming to uplift the homeless, providing them not just with essentials but skills, training, and emotional support. He often shared with his peers, "*True success isn't just in what we accumulate, but in what we give back. Remember the Good Samaritan; it's not about religion but humanity. You got this.*"

Months turned into years, and Jake's foundation impacted thousands. Yet, the most significant change was in Jake himself. He often sat in his penthouse, overlooking the city, reflecting on his journey from self-centeredness to service. He realized that in serving others, he had found a higher purpose, a divine calling, and an immeasurable joy.

Examples of Negative Self-Talk for "Service & Philanthropy"

"I don't have enough to give."

"What difference can I make?"

"Charity doesn't change anything."

"I've got my own problems to deal with."

"People should help themselves."

"I gave once, and it was misused."

"There's no real joy in giving."

"Philanthropy is for the super-rich."

"I'll think about giving back when I have more."

"Charities are just businesses in disguise."

Alright, let's dig a little deeper. What negative self-talk have you caught yourself saying or heard others say? This is your chance to confront those limiting beliefs head-on. Jot down your thoughts right here, or flip to the extra pages at the end of the book to really dive in. You got this—let's keep winning and turning those negative thoughts into positive vibes. God bless.

....

....

....

....

....

Reflection Questions

"When was the last time I selflessly helped someone, expecting nothing in return?"

"How do I define true success in my life?"

"What legacy do I wish to leave behind?"

"How can I incorporate service into my daily routine?"

"What's stopping me from taking the first step towards philanthropy?"

Dive into these reflection questions and let your thoughts flow. Whether you jot down your answers right here or flip to the extra pages at the end of the book, make this space your own. You got this—let's keep winning. God bless.

....

....

....

....

....

....

....

....

....

....

Service and Philanthropy

STEPS	BOX LABEL	DESCRIPTION &EXAMPLES
Step 1	**Recognize Negative Patterns"**	The first step is to become aware of any negative self-talk or actions that are hindering your involvement in service and philanthropy. **Examples:** "I don't have enough time to volunteer," "My small donation won't make a difference," "I'm not good enough to contribute meaningfully."
Step 2	**Find the Root**	Dig deep to identify the root cause of your negative self-talk or actions. Is it fear, past experiences, or a lack of self-worth? **Examples:** Fear of judgment, feeling overwhelmed, past failures.
Step 3	**Challenge & Reframe**	Actively challenge your negative thoughts or actions. Reframe them into positive affirmations or constructive actions. **Examples:** "My time is valuable, and giving it to a cause means a lot," "Every contribution counts," "I have unique skills that can help others."
Step 4	**Initiate Positive Action**	Use your newly framed positive affirmations to guide you in taking concrete steps towards service and philanthropy. **Examples:** Sign up for a volunteer event, make a small donation, offer your skills to a non-profit.
Step 5	**Cultivate Better Habits**	Make a commitment to regularly engage in actions that align with your goals in service and philanthropy. This will help establish better habits over time. **Examples:** Set a monthly volunteering schedule, automate charitable donations, join a community service group.

Positive Affirmations / Self-Talk for "Service & Philanthropy"

1. *"Today, I choose to serve with an open heart."*

2. *"Every act of kindness creates ripples of change."*

3. *"I am blessed to be a blessing to others."*

4. *"Philanthropy is my way of giving back to the universe."*

5. *"In serving others, I find my true purpose."*

6. *"Every penny I give brings joy tenfold."*

7. *"Let's keep winning by lifting others up."*

8. *"I am a vessel of change and love."*

9. *"God blesses me so I can bless others."*

10. *"Service is the highest form of gratitude."*

11. *"I am empowered to make a difference."*

12. *"Every hand I extend in help builds bridges of hope."*

13. *"Philanthropy is not about wealth; it's about heart."*

14. *"I am destined to serve and uplift."*

15. *"The joy of giving surpasses the joy of receiving."*

16. *"I got this, and I've got others too."*

17. *"Every act of service is a step towards a better world."*

18. *"I am a beacon of hope and love."*

19. *"God bless my intentions to serve selflessly."*

20. *"Let's keep winning by spreading kindness."*

21. *"I am aligned with the universe's plan of service."*

22. "Philanthropy is my soul's calling."

23. "I am enriched when I enrich others."

24. "Service is my way of saying thank you to the universe."

25. "Every day, I find new ways to make a difference."

26. "I am a catalyst for positive change."

27. "God bless every hand that serves."

28. "Let's keep winning by sharing our blessings."

29. "I am divinely guided in my acts of charity."

30. "Philanthropy is the echo of love in action."

31. "I got this, and I'll ensure others do too."

32. "Service is the melody of the soul."

33. "Every smile I bring is a reward in itself."

34. "God bless my journey of giving."

35. "Let's keep winning by touching lives."

36. "I am a powerhouse of love and service."

37. "Philanthropy is the art of the heart."

38. "I am destined to make the world a better place."

39. "Service is my silent prayer."

40. "Every act of kindness is a step closer to God."

41. "I got this gift of giving."

42. "Let's keep winning by being the change."

43. "I am a messenger of hope and love."

44. "Philanthropy is my heart's true calling."

45. *"God bless every penny I give."*

46. *"Service is my way of echoing divine love."*

47. *"I am a torchbearer of change."*

48. *"Every hand I help strengthens my soul."*

49. *"Let's keep winning by spreading joy."*

50. *"I am aligned with the universe's philanthropic pulse."*

51. *"Service is my spiritual practice."*

52. *"I got this heart that beats for others."*

53. *"Philanthropy is my soul's dance."*

54. *"Every act of service is a hug to humanity."*

55. *"God bless every soul I touch."*

56. *"Let's keep winning by being there for others."*

57. *"I am a mirror of love and kindness."*

58. *"Philanthropy is my way of echoing God's love."*

59. *"Service is my silent anthem."*

60. *"Every smile I spread is a blessing counted."*

61. *"I got this spirit of endless giving."*

62. *"Let's keep winning by sharing love."*

63. *"I am a vessel of God's endless love."*

64. *"Philanthropy is my heart's song."*

65. *"Service is my way of saying I care."*

66. *"Every penny I give is a prayer answered."*

67. *"God bless my journey of endless service."*

68. *"Let's keep winning by being God's hands."*

69. *"I am a channel of divine love."*

70. *"Philanthropy is my soul's whisper."*

71. *"Service is my way of echoing the universe's love."*

72. *"Every act of kindness is a star in my crown."*

73. *"I got this spirit of boundless love."*

74. *"Let's keep winning by being the light."*

75. *"I am a reflection of God's endless love."*

76. *"Philanthropy is my heart's echo."*

77. *"Service is my silent sermon."*

78. *"Every hand I hold is a blessing earned."*

79. *"God bless my spirit of giving."*

80. *"Let's keep winning by holding hands."*

81. *"I am a beacon of God's love."*

82. *"Philanthropy is my soul's embrace."*

83. *"Service is my way of touching souls."*

84. *"Every smile I share is a prayer echoed."*

85. *"I got this heart of gold."*

86. *"Let's keep winning by sharing warmth."*

87. *"I am a reflection of the universe's love."*

88. *"Philanthropy is my heart's prayer."*

89. *"Service is my silent chant."*

90. *"Every act of love is a step towards divinity."*

91. *"God bless my path of service."*

92. *"Let's keep winning by being angels on earth."*

93. *"I am a messenger of the universe's love."*

94. *"Philanthropy is my soul's sigh."*

95. *"Service is my way of being God's echo."*

96. *"Every penny shared is a blessing doubled."*

97. *"I got this spirit of divine love."*

98. *"Let's keep winning by being love incarnate."*

99. *"I am a vessel of the universe's blessings."*

100. *"Philanthropy is my heart's beat."*

101. *"Service is my silent vow."*

102. *"Every act of service is a divine echo."*

103. *"God bless my heart of service."*

104. *"Let's keep winning by being love's echo."*

105. *"I am a torchbearer of the universe's love."*

106. *"Philanthropy is my soul's touch."*

107. *"Service is my silent promise."*

108. *"Every hand extended is a blessing earned."*

109. *"I got this spirit of boundless service."*

110. *"Let's keep winning by being love's reflection."*

111. *"I am a mirror of the universe's blessings."*

112. *"Philanthropy is my heart's voice."*

113. *"Service is my silent pledge."*

114. *"Every smile shared is a divine touch."*

115. *"God bless my endless journey of giving."*

116. *"Let's keep winning by being blessings."*

117. *"I am a beacon of the universe's touch."*

118. *"Philanthropy is my soul's voice."*

119. *"Service is my silent commitment."*

120. *"Every act of love is a divine whisper."*

121. *"I got this heart of boundless blessings."*

122. *"Let's keep winning by being the universe's voice."*

123. *"I am a reflection of divine love."*

124. *"Philanthropy is my heart's touch."*

125. *"Service is my silent word."*

126. *"Every penny given is a divine echo."*

127. *"God bless my spirit of boundless blessings."*

128. *"Let's keep winning by being love's voice."*

129. *"I am a vessel of divine touch."*

130. *"Philanthropy is my soul's song."*

131. *"Service is my silent oath."*

132. *"Every hand held is a divine touch."*

133. *"I got this spirit of endless blessings."*

134. *"Let's keep winning by being the universe's song."*

135. *"I am a beacon of divine blessings."*

136. *"Philanthropy is my heart's sigh."*

137. *"Service is my silent word."*

138. *"Every smile given is a divine song."*

139. *"God bless my journey of boundless love."*

140. *"Let's keep winning by being blessings on earth."*

141. *"I am a reflection of divine touch."*

142. *"Philanthropy is my soul's touch."*

143. *"Service is my silent commitment."*

144. *"Every penny shared is a divine whisper."*

145. *"I got this heart of endless love."*

146. *"Let's keep winning by being the universe's touch."*

147. *"I am a vessel of divine blessings."*

148. *"Philanthropy is my heart's whisper."*

149. *"Service is my silent promise."*

150. *"Every act of service is a divine promise."*

Remember, in giving, we receive. In serving, we find our true purpose. Life's true essence is in giving, in serving, and in loving. Let's keep winning, not just for ourselves but for all. Dive deep, reflect, and find that Good Samaritan within. You got this. God bless.

Social Confidence

"Believe in yourself and there will come a day when others will have no choice but to believe with you."
- Cynthia Kersey

"Each time we face our fear, we gain strength, courage, and confidence in the doing."
- Theodore Roosevelt

"Confidence is contagious. Catch it. Spread it."
- Anonymous

"Your energy introduces you before you even speak."
- Anonymous

"Speak with honesty, think with sincerity, act with integrity."
- Anonymous

The Gathering: Embracing the Light Within

In the age of social media, where every interaction is a click away, many find themselves more isolated than ever. The concept of social confidence isn't just about speaking up; it's about recognizing the divine light within us and understanding that we are all interconnected through this divine tapestry.

James was a modern-day introvert. He loved his small circle of friends but dreaded social gatherings. The thought of mingling with strangers or speaking up in a group was paralyzing. One day, he stumbled upon the biblical story of Moses. Despite being a stutterer, Moses was chosen by God to lead a nation. He wasn't the most eloquent, but he had a divine purpose. Inspired, James decided to attend a community gathering. As he entered, he felt like a fish out of water. But then he remembered Moses and whispered to himself, "Let's keep winning." He approached a group, introduced himself, and shared his passion for art. To his surprise, a lady in the group was an art enthusiast, and they connected instantly. That evening, James didn't just make a new friend; he discovered the power of shared passions and the beauty of divine connections. With his newfound confidence, James penned down affirmations to boost his social confidence:

"I am a beacon of light, attracting like-minded souls."

"Every interaction is a divine appointment."

"I am worthy of meaningful connections."

"My voice matters, and my story is important."

"I embrace every opportunity to shine my light."

James began sharing his journey with others. "*Start small*," he'd advise. "*Find gatherings around your passions. Remember, it's not about impressing; it's about expressing. Share a bit of yourself, and you'll find others doing the same. And always remember, you got this.*"

As months turned into years, James transformed from an introvert to a confident social butterfly, not because he changed who he was, but because he embraced it. He often reflected on his journey, the fears he overcame, and the connections he made. And in those moments of introspection, he realized that every individual he met was a reflection of a part of him, teaching him, guiding him, and enriching his life.

Examples of Negative Self-Talk for "Social Confidence"

"I'm too awkward to fit in."

"People will find me boring."

"I always say the wrong things."

"No one will remember me."

"I'm better off alone."

"I'm not interesting enough."

"They're probably laughing at me."

"I'll just embarrass myself."

"I don't belong here."

"Why would they want to talk to me?"

Alright, let's dig a little deeper. What negative self-talk have you caught yourself saying or heard others say? This is your chance to confront those limiting beliefs head-on. Jot down your thoughts right here, or flip to the extra pages at the end of the book to really dive in. You got this—let's keep winning and turning those negative thoughts into positive vibes. God bless.

....

....

....

....

....

Reflection Questions

"When was the last time I stepped out of my comfort zone in a social setting, and what did I learn?"

"What are the qualities I bring to a social interaction?"

"How do my beliefs about myself influence my social interactions?"

"What common interests can I use as a bridge to connect with others?"

"How can I challenge one negative belief about my social skills this week?"

Dive into these reflection questions and let your thoughts flow. Whether you jot down your answers right here or flip to the extra pages at the end of the book, make this space your own. You got this—let's keep winning. God bless.

....

....

....

....

....

....

....

....

....

....

Social Confidence

STEPS NO.	STEPS	DESCRIPTION &EXAMPLES
Step 1	**Identify Negative Self-Talk or Actions**	Recognize the negative self-talk or actions that are hindering your social confidence. **Example Phrases:** "I'm too awkward to talk to new people," "I'll embarrass myself," "I'm not interesting."
Step 2	**Trace the Root Cause**	Dig deep to find the underlying reason for this negative self-talk or behavior. Is it past experiences, fear of judgment, or something else? **Questions to Ask:** "Why do I feel this way?", "When did this start?", "What triggers these thoughts?"
Step 3	**Challenge and Reframe**	Challenge these negative thoughts by questioning their validity and reframing them into positive affirmations. **Example:** Turn "I'm too awkward" into "I bring a unique perspective into social situations."
Step 4	**Implement New Habits**	Take actionable steps to improve your social confidence. This could be practicing your affirmations, engaging in social activities, or seeking advice. **Action Items:** Attend a social event, practice active listening, or engage in small talk with a stranger.
Step 5	**Reflect and Adjust**	After a set period, reflect on your progress. Have your thoughts and actions aligned better with your goal of improved social confidence? **Questions to Ask:** "Do I feel more confident?", "What worked?", "What needs adjustment?"

Positive Affirmations / Self-Talk for "Social Confidence"

1. *"Every interaction is a chance to shine. I embrace it."*

2. *"I am a magnet for positive social experiences."*

3. *"With every breath, I grow more confident in social settings."*

4. *"I've faced challenges before and conquered them. Social situations are no different."*

5. *"Every conversation is an opportunity to learn and grow."*

6. *"I bring value to every social interaction."*

7. *"God has blessed me with a unique voice, and I'm not afraid to use it."*

8. *"I deserve meaningful and positive connections."*

9. *"Every day, I become more comfortable in my own skin."*

10. *"I've got this. Every social challenge is an opportunity in disguise."*

11. *"I am the master of my feelings, and today, I choose confidence."*

12. *"I am surrounded by love and understanding, even in a crowd."*

13. *"Social settings are my playground. I thrive in them."*

14. *"I am a beacon of light and positivity in every room I enter."*

15. *"I trust in my ability to communicate effectively and authentically."*

16. *"God blesses every word I speak, making my conversations fruitful."*

17. *"I am worthy of being heard and understood."*

18. *"Every interaction strengthens my social muscles."*

19. *"I am in control of my social destiny."*

20. *"Let's keep winning, one conversation at a time."*

21. "I am not defined by one awkward moment but by countless positive ones."

22. "I bring joy, insight, and warmth to every conversation."

23. "I am resilient. Social setbacks only propel me forward."

24. "My confidence is a gift, and I share it generously."

25. "I am a social warrior, ready to conquer any challenge."

26. "Every person I meet adds to my tapestry of experiences."

27. "I am blessed with the gift of gab and the heart to listen."

28. "I deserve deep and meaningful connections."

29. "I am a master at navigating social waters with grace."

30. "Every day, I am more at ease with myself and others."

31. "I am a positive force in every social setting."

32. "I am blessed with the ability to connect and understand."

33. "I am confident, capable, and charismatic."

34. "I am a magnet for positive interactions and friendships."

35. "I deserve love, respect, and understanding in every conversation."

36. "I am a beacon of confidence and authenticity."

37. "I am blessed with social wisdom and understanding."

38. "Every conversation is a step closer to my best self."

39. "I am a master of my emotions and reactions."

40. "I deserve being seen and heard."

41. "I am a social butterfly, spreading joy wherever I go."

42. "I am a reflection of God's love in every interaction."

43. *"I am a powerhouse of confidence and charm."*

44. *"I am blessed with the gift of connection."*

45. *"I am a beacon of positivity in every group."*

46. *"I am a master of social dynamics and interactions."*

47. *"I deserve every compliment and kind word."*

48. *"I am a magnet for positive social experiences."*

49. *"I am a reflection of God's grace in every conversation."*

50. *"I am a master of my social destiny."*

51. *"I deserve love and understanding in every setting."*

52. *"I am a powerhouse of social wisdom and grace."*

53. *"I am a beacon of light in every room."*

54. *"I am a reflection of God's love in every interaction."*

55. *"I am a magnet for meaningful connections."*

56. *"I am a powerhouse of social confidence and charm."*

57. *"I deserve respect and understanding."*

58. *"I am a beacon of positivity in every conversation."*

59. *"I am a reflection of God's grace in every setting."*

60. *"I am a magnet for positive interactions and friendships."*

61. *"I am a powerhouse of social wisdom and understanding."*

62. *"I deserve every kind word and gesture."*

63. *"I am a beacon of light in every social setting."*

64. *"I am a reflection of God's love in every conversation."*

65. *"I am a magnet for love and understanding."*

66. *"I am a powerhouse of confidence and authenticity."*

67. *"I deserve deep and meaningful connections."*

68. *"I am a beacon of positivity in every room."*

69. *"I am a reflection of God's grace in every interaction."*

70. *"I am a magnet for positive experiences and connections."*

71. *"I am a powerhouse of social charm and grace."*

72. *"I deserve love and respect in every setting."*

73. *"I am a beacon of light in every conversation."*

74. *"I am a reflection of God's love in every room."*

75. *"I am a magnet for positive interactions and friendships."*

76. *"I am a powerhouse of social wisdom and charm."*

77. *"I deserve every compliment and kind gesture."*

78. *"I am a beacon of positivity in every setting."*

79. *"I am a reflection of God's grace in every conversation."*

80. *"I am a magnet for love and understanding."*

81. *"I am a powerhouse of confidence and authenticity."*

82. *"I deserve deep and meaningful connections."*

83. *"I am a beacon of light in every room."*

84. *"I am a reflection of God's love in every interaction."*

85. *"I am a magnet for positive experiences and connections."*

86. *"I am a powerhouse of social charm and grace."*

87. *"I deserve love and respect in every conversation."*

88. *"I am a beacon of positivity in every setting."*

89. "I am a reflection of God's grace in every room."

90. "I am a magnet for positive interactions and friendships."

91. "I am a powerhouse of social wisdom and charm."

92. "I deserve every kind word and compliment."

93. "I am a beacon of light in every conversation."

94. "I am a reflection of God's love in every setting."

95. "I am a magnet for love and understanding."

96. "I am a powerhouse of confidence and authenticity."

97. "I deserve deep and meaningful connections."

98. "I am a beacon of positivity in every room."

99. "I am a reflection of God's grace in every interaction."

100. "I am a magnet for positive experiences and connections."

101. "I am a powerhouse of social charm and grace."

102. "I deserve love and respect in every setting."

103. "I am a beacon of light in every conversation."

104. "I am a reflection of God's love in every room."

105. "I am a magnet for positive interactions and friendships."

106. "I am a powerhouse of social wisdom and charm."

107. "I deserve every compliment and kind gesture."

108. "I am a beacon of positivity in every setting."

109. "I am a reflection of God's grace in every conversation."

110. "I am a magnet for love and understanding."

111. "I am a powerhouse of confidence and authenticity."

112. *"I deserve deep and meaningful connections."*

113. *"I am a beacon of light in every room."*

114. *"I am a reflection of God's love in every interaction."*

115. *"I am a magnet for positive experiences and connections."*

116. *"I am a powerhouse of social charm and grace."*

117. *"I deserve love and respect in every conversation."*

118. *"I am a beacon of positivity in every setting."*

119. *"I am a reflection of God's grace in every room."*

120. *"I am a magnet for positive interactions and friendships."*

121. *"I am a powerhouse of social wisdom and charm."*

122. *"I deserve every kind word and compliment."*

123. *"I am a beacon of light in every conversation."*

124. *"I am a reflection of God's love in every setting."*

125. *"I am a magnet for love and understanding."*

126. *"I am a powerhouse of confidence and authenticity."*

127. *"I deserve deep and meaningful connections."*

128. *"I am a beacon of positivity in every room."*

129. *"I am a reflection of God's grace in every interaction."*

130. *"I am a magnet for positive experiences and connections."*

131. *"I am a powerhouse of social charm and grace."*

132. *"I deserve love and respect in every setting."*

133. *"I am a beacon of light in every conversation."*

134. *"I am a reflection of God's love in every room."*

135. *"I am a magnet for positive interactions and friendships."*

136. *"I am a powerhouse of social wisdom and charm."*

137. *"I deserve every compliment and kind gesture."*

138. *"I am a beacon of positivity in every setting."*

139. *"I am a reflection of God's grace in every conversation."*

140. *"I am a magnet for love and understanding."*

141. *"I am a powerhouse of confidence and authenticity."*

142. *"I deserve deep and meaningful connections."*

143. *"I am a beacon of light in every room."*

144. *"I am a reflection of God's love in every interaction."*

145. *"I am a magnet for positive experiences and connections."*

146. *"I am a powerhouse of social charm and grace."*

147. *"I deserve love and respect in every conversation."*

148. *"I am a beacon of positivity in every setting."*

149. *"I am a reflection of God's grace in every room."*

150. *"I am a magnet for positive interactions and friendships."*

Remember, let's keep winning in every social setting. Life is a series of divine connections waiting to happen. Embrace them, cherish them, and let your light shine. Let's keep winning together. God bless.

Spiritual Connection

"Spiritual connection does not come from religion, but from deep within oneself."
- Anonymous

"To touch the soul of another human being is to walk on holy ground."
- Stephen R. Covey

"The spiritual journey is the unlearning of fear and the acceptance of love."
- Marianne Williamson

"Faith is the bird that feels the light when the dawn is still dark."
- Rabindranath Tagore

"The soul has been given its own ears to hear things the mind does not understand."
- Rumi

The Digital Desert: Finding the Oasis of Spiritual Connection

In our 21st-century world, where technology reigns supreme, and our attention is constantly divided among devices, notifications, and digital obligations, the quest for a deeper spiritual connection has never been more challenging yet profoundly essential. The biblical principle of seeking solitude in the wilderness to find God echoes in our modern lives, urging us to find our own spiritual oasis amidst the digital desert.

Jacob was a tech-savvy millennial, always connected, always online. His life revolved around his devices, from work meetings on Zoom to socializing on various apps. But amidst this digital whirlwind, he felt an emptiness, a yearning for something more profound. One day, while scrolling through his feed, he stumbled upon a quote from the Bible, "*Be still, and know that I am God.*" It struck a chord. Inspired, he decided to embark on a digital detox, a modern-day version of Jesus' 40 days in the desert. He ventured to a cabin in the woods, leaving behind his devices, seeking spiritual clarity. In the silence of nature, Jacob began to feel a connection he had never felt before. He realized that just as Moses found God in the burning bush in the desert's solitude, he was also finding his spiritual connection in the quiet of the woods, away from the digital chaos. With a renewed sense of purpose, Jacob began his days with affirmations that grounded him:

"In the silence, I hear the whispers of the Divine."

"I am connected, not by Wi-Fi, but by the spiritual bond I share with the Creator."

"Every moment of stillness brings me closer to my true self and the Divine."

"Let's keep winning by nurturing our souls as much as our digital profiles."

"In every pause, I find God waiting for me."

Returning to the city, Jacob felt transformed. He began sharing his experience, advising friends to take digital breaks, even if just for an hour. "Find your burning bush moment," he'd say. "*It might not be in the woods, but perhaps in a quiet corner of your home or a peaceful park. Disconnect to truly connect. You got this.*"

As days turned into weeks, Jacob often found himself reflecting on his time in the woods. He realized spiritual connection wasn't about grand gestures but daily, intentional moments of seeking the Divine. He began journaling, capturing his thoughts, his struggles, and his moments of spiritual epiphany.

Examples of Negative Self-Talk for "Spiritual Connection"

"I'm too busy to find time for spirituality."

"I'm not spiritual enough."

"Maybe I'm just not meant to have a deep connection with the Divine."

"I've done too many wrongs for God to care about me."

"Spirituality doesn't have a place in the modern world."

"I feel disconnected and lost."

"I've tried, but I just don't feel anything."

"Maybe I'm just not chosen or special."

"I don't understand all these spiritual texts and teachings."

"It's too hard to find silence in this noisy world."

Alright, let's dig a little deeper. What negative self-talk have you caught yourself saying or heard others say? This is your chance to confront those limiting beliefs head-on. Jot down your thoughts right here, or flip to the extra pages at the end of the book to really dive in. You got this—let's keep winning and turning those negative thoughts into positive vibes. God bless.

....

....

....

....

....

Reflection Questions

"When was the last time I truly felt a deep spiritual connection, and what triggered it?"

"What digital distractions most often pull me away from my spiritual journey?"

"How can I create a daily ritual that prioritizes my spiritual well-being?"

"What does a meaningful spiritual connection look like to me?"

"How can I bring the peace and clarity I find in moments of spirituality into my daily life?"

Dive into these reflection questions and let your thoughts flow. Whether you jot down your answers right here or flip to the extra pages at the end of the book, make this space your own. You got this—let's keep winning. God bless.

....

....

....

....

....

....

....

....

....

Spiritual Connection

STEPS NO.	STEPS	DESCRIPTION &EXAMPLES
Step 1	Identify Negative Self-Talk or Actions	Recognize the negative self-talk or actions that are hindering your spiritual connection. **Example:** "I don't have time for spiritual practices," "I'm not spiritual enough," or skipping meditation/prayer sessions.
Step 2	Trace the Root Cause	Dig deep to find the underlying reason for the negative self-talk or actions. **Example:** Lack of time management, past negative experiences with spirituality, or societal influences.
Step 3	Challenge and Reframe	Challenge the negative self-talk and reframe it into a positive affirmation. **Example:** Change "I don't have time for spiritual practices" to "I make time for what nourishes my soul."
Step 4	Implement Positive Affirmations and Actions	Start incorporating the positive affirmations into your daily routine and take small actions that align with them. **Example:** Set aside 5 minutes each day for prayer or meditation, and repeat the affirmation: "I am spiritually connected and at peace."
Step 5	Monitor and Adjust	Keep track of your progress. Are you feeling more spiritually connected? If not, adjust your affirmations or actions. **Example:** Use a spiritual journal to note any changes in your feelings of spiritual connection, and adjust your practices accordingly.

Positive Affirmations / Self-Talk for "Spiritual Connection"

1. *"I am fearfully and wonderfully made, a masterpiece of the Creator. - Inspired by Psalm 139:14."*

2. *"God's plans for me are for good, to give me a future and hope. - Inspired by Jeremiah 29:11."*

3. *"I am more than a conqueror through Him who loves me. - Inspired by Romans 8:37."*

4. *"The Lord is my shepherd; I shall not want. - Inspired by Psalm 23:1."*

5. *"I am the light of the world, shining bright amidst the darkness. - Inspired by Matthew 5:14."*

6. *"I am God's handiwork, created for good works. - Inspired by Ephesians 2:10."*

7. *"The joy of the Lord is my strength. - Inspired by Nehemiah 8:10."*

8. *"I am blessed and highly favored. - Inspired by Luke 1:28."*

9. *"God's grace is sufficient for me. - Inspired by 2 Corinthians 12:9."*

10. *"I am a child of God, loved and cherished. - Inspired by John 1:12."*

11. *"I am the head and not the tail, above and not beneath. - Inspired by Deuteronomy 28:13."*

12. *"I am chosen, royal, and holy, God's special possession. - Inspired by 1 Peter 2:9."*

13. *"I am redeemed and forgiven. - Inspired by Ephesians 1:7."*

14. *"I am a temple of the Holy Spirit. - Inspired by 1 Corinthians 6:19."*

15. *"I am rooted and established in love. - Inspired by Ephesians 3:17."*

16. *"I am a friend of Jesus. - Inspired by John 15:15."*

17. "I am seated with Christ in heavenly places. - Inspired by Ephesians 2:6."

18. "I am the salt of the earth, adding flavor wherever I go. - Inspired by Matthew 5:13."

19. "I am an overcomer by the blood of the Lamb. - Inspired by Revelation 12:11."

20. "I am a branch of the true vine, bearing much fruit. - Inspired by John 15:1-5."

21. "I am a co-heir with Christ. - Inspired by Romans 8:17."

22. "I am God's workmanship, His poetry in motion. - Inspired by Ephesians 2:10."

23. "I am a new creation; the old has passed away. - Inspired by 2 Corinthians 5:17."

24. "I am strong in the Lord and in His mighty power. - Inspired by Ephesians 6:10."

25. "I am filled with the peace of God that surpasses understanding. - Inspired by Philippians 4:7."

26. "I am an ambassador for Christ. - Inspired by 2 Corinthians 5:20."

27. "I am clothed with strength and dignity. - Inspired by Proverbs 31:25."

28. "I am complete in Christ. - Inspired by Colossians 2:10."

29. "I am chosen by God, set apart for His purpose. - Inspired by Ephesians 1:4."

30. "I am steadfast, immovable, always abounding in God's work. - Inspired by 1 Corinthians 15:58."

31. "I am a light in the world, reflecting God's glory. - Inspired by Matthew 5:14."

32. "I am called according to God's purpose. - Inspired by Romans 8:28."

33. *"I am shielded by God's power. - Inspired by 1 Peter 1:5."*

34. *"I am free from condemnation. - Inspired by Romans 8:1."*

35. *"I am a city set on a hill, shining bright for all to see. - Inspired by Matthew 5:14."*

36. *"I am the righteousness of God in Christ. - Inspired by 2 Corinthians 5:21."*

37. *"I am anointed and sealed by God. - Inspired by 2 Corinthians 1:21-22."*

38. *"I am chosen and appointed to bear fruit. - Inspired by John 15:16."*

39. *"I am a partaker of His divine nature. - Inspired by 2 Peter 1:4."*

40. *"I am an heir of God's glory. - Inspired by Romans 8:17."*

41. *"I am a living stone, being built up in Christ. - Inspired by 1 Peter 2:5."*

42. *"I am God's treasured possession. - Inspired by Deuteronomy 7:6."*

43. *"I am delivered from the powers of darkness. - Inspired by Colossians 1:13."*

44. *"I am led by the Spirit of God. - Inspired by Romans 8:14."*

45. *"I am kept in perfect peace because I trust in Him. - Inspired by Isaiah 26:3."*

46. *"I am confident that God will complete the work He started in me. - Inspired by Philippians 1:6."*

47. *"I am a member of God's royal priesthood. - Inspired by 1 Peter 2:9."*

48. *"I am the apple of God's eye. - Inspired by Psalm 17:8."*

49. *"I am blessed with every spiritual blessing in Christ. - Inspired by Ephesians 1:3."*

50. *"I am chosen to proclaim His excellencies. - Inspired by 1 Peter 2:9."*

51. *"I am surrounded by God's favor wherever I go. - Inspired by Psalm 5:12."*

52. *"I am steadfast in faith, knowing God is by my side. - Inspired by 1 Corinthians 16:13."*

53. *"I am walking by faith, not by sight. - Inspired by 2 Corinthians 5:7."*

54. *"I am filled with the fruits of righteousness. - Inspired by Philippians 1:11."*

55. *"I am a vessel for God's glory. - Inspired by Romans 9:23."*

56. *"I am not anxious, for I cast all my cares on Him. - Inspired by 1 Peter 5:7."*

57. *"I am walking in the path God has set for me. - Inspired by Psalm 119:105."*

58. *"I am a beacon of hope and love in this world. - Inspired by Matthew 5:16."*

59. *"I am deeply loved by the Father. - Inspired by 1 John 3:1."*

60. *"I am protected under the shadow of His wings. - Inspired by Psalm 91:1."*

61. *"I am not shaken, for God is my refuge. - Inspired by Psalm 62:6."*

62. *"I am filled with the wisdom of God. - Inspired by James 1:5."*

63. *"I am a peacemaker, blessed and called a child of God. - Inspired by Matthew 5:9."*

64. *"I am strengthened with might through His Spirit. - Inspired by Ephesians 3:16."*

65. *"I am a witness of God's power and love. - Inspired by Acts 1:8."*

66. *"I am a disciple of Christ, spreading His teachings. - Inspired by Matthew 28:19."*

67. "I am clothed in the armor of God. - Inspired by Ephesians 6:11."

68. "I am a channel of God's blessings. - Inspired by Genesis 12:2."

69. "I am triumphant in Christ. - Inspired by 2 Corinthians 2:14."

70. "I am not alone; God is always with me. - Inspired by Isaiah 41:10."

71. "I am living in abundance, for God supplies all my needs. - Inspired by Philippians 4:19."

72. "I am a reflection of God's glory. - Inspired by 2 Corinthians 3:18."

73. "I am a doer of the Word, blessed in all my actions. - Inspired by James 1:22."

74. "I am set free from any bondage. - Inspired by John 8:36."

75. "I am walking in the Spirit, producing its fruit. - Inspired by Galatians 5:22-23."

76. "I am a light, shining in the darkness. - Inspired by John 1:5."

77. "I am chosen by God, even before the world began. - Inspired by Ephesians 1:4."

78. "I am filled with joy unspeakable and full of glory. - Inspired by 1 Peter 1:8."

79. "I am a part of the body of Christ. - Inspired by 1 Corinthians 12:27."

80. "I am a citizen of heaven. - Inspired by Philippians 3:20."

81. "I am the fragrance of Christ to God. - Inspired by 2 Corinthians 2:15."

82. "I am a letter from Christ, written by the Spirit. - Inspired by 2 Corinthians 3:3."

83. "I am blessed when I come in and when I go out. - Inspired by Deuteronomy 28:6."

84. "I am a friend of God. - Inspired by James 2:23."

85. "I am established in righteousness. - Inspired by Isaiah 54:14."

86. "I am an heir to the blessings of Abraham. - Inspired by Galatians 3:14."

87. "I am the righteousness of God in Christ. - Inspired by 2 Corinthians 5:21."

88. "I am a house of prayer. - Inspired by Isaiah 56:7."

89. "I am a living sacrifice, holy and acceptable to God. - Inspired by Romans 12:1."

90. "I am a partaker of the heavenly calling. - Inspired by Hebrews 3:1."

91. "I am the salt of the earth. - Inspired by Matthew 5:13."

92. "I am a branch connected to the true vine. - Inspired by John 15:5."

93. "I am a worker together with God. - Inspired by 1 Corinthians 3:9."

94. "I am the clay in the Potter's hands. - Inspired by Isaiah 64:8."

95. "I am a royal diadem in the hand of God. - Inspired by Isaiah 62:3."

96. "I am a crown of beauty and a royal priesthood. - Inspired by 1 Peter 2:9."

97. "I am a chosen generation, proclaiming His praises. - Inspired by 1 Peter 2:9."

98. "I am a son/daughter of the Most High. - Inspired by Psalm 82:6."

99. "I am a joint heir with Christ. - Inspired by Romans 8:17."

100. "I am the temple of the Holy Spirit. - Inspired by 1 Corinthians 6:19."

101. "I am rooted and grounded in love. - Inspired by Ephesians 3:17."

102. "I am more than a conqueror through Christ. - Inspired by Romans 8:37."

103. "I am a beacon of God's love and light. - Inspired by Matthew 5:14."

104. *"I am a reflection of God's heart. - Inspired by Genesis 1:27."*

105. *"I am shielded by God's promises. - Inspired by 2 Peter 1:4."*

106. *"I am destined for greatness in His kingdom. - Inspired by Jeremiah 29:11."*

107. *"I am not moved by the world, for my foundation is in Christ. - Inspired by 1 Corinthians 3:11."*

108. *"I am always in God's care and under His guidance. - Inspired by Psalm 32:8."*

109. *"I am constantly renewed by His grace. - Inspired by 2 Corinthians 4:16."*

110. *"I am a vessel of His peace and love. - Inspired by 1 John 4:16."*

111. *"I am empowered by His word. - Inspired by Hebrews 4:12."*

112. *"I am not bound by the past; I am a new creation. - Inspired by 2 Corinthians 5:17."*

113. *"I am walking in divine purpose. - Inspired by Proverbs 19:21."*

114. *"I am shielded by His everlasting love. - Inspired by Romans 8:38-39."*

115. *"I am not fearful, for He is with me. - Inspired by Isaiah 41:10."*

116. *"I am always in the overflow of His blessings. - Inspired by Malachi 3:10."*

117. *"I am a testimony of His endless mercy. - Inspired by Lamentations 3:22-23."*

118. *"I am filled with the spirit of wisdom and revelation. - Inspired by Ephesians 1:17."*

119. *"I am a doer of the Word, and I am blessed. - Inspired by James 1:25."*

120. *"I am walking in divine health. - Inspired by 3 John 1:2."*

121. "I am surrounded by angels who guard me. - Inspired by Psalm 91:11."

122. "I am always in alignment with God's will. - Inspired by Romans 12:2."

123. "I am a magnet for divine favor. - Inspired by Psalm 84:11."

124. "I am a living testimony of His power. - Inspired by Acts 1:8."

125. "I am always under the shadow of the Almighty. - Inspired by Psalm 91:1."

126. "I am a carrier of His joy and peace. - Inspired by Romans 15:13."

127. "I am a beacon of hope in a world that needs Him. - Inspired by Romans 15:13."

128. "I am a channel of His miracles. - Inspired by John 14:12."

129. "I am always in tune with His voice. - Inspired by John 10:27."

130. "I am a manifestation of His promises. - Inspired by 2 Corinthians 1:20."

131. "I am a warrior in His kingdom. - Inspired by Ephesians 6:11."

132. "I am a disciple, spreading His word. - Inspired by Matthew 28:19."

133. "I am a seeker of His kingdom first. - Inspired by Matthew 6:33."

134. "I am a holder of the keys to His kingdom. - Inspired by Matthew 16:19."

135. "I am a pursuer of His righteousness. - Inspired by Matthew 5:6."

136. "I am a reflection of His grace. - Inspired by Ephesians 2:8."

137. "I am a bearer of the fruit of the Spirit. - Inspired by Galatians 5:22-23."

138. "I am a living sacrifice for His glory. - Inspired by Romans 12:1."

139. "I am a seeker and knower of His truth. - Inspired by John 8:32."

140. *"I am a worshiper in spirit and truth. - Inspired by John 4:24."*

141. *"I am a vessel of honor in His house. - Inspired by 2 Timothy 2:21."*

142. *"I am a partaker of His divine nature. - Inspired by 2 Peter 1:4."*

143. *"I am a believer, and all things are possible for me. - Inspired by Mark 9:23."*

144. *"I am a child of the King, and I walk in authority. - Inspired by Luke 10:19."*

145. *"I am a follower of Christ, and I shall not want. - Inspired by Psalm 23:1."*

146. *"I am a beacon of His unconditional love. - Inspired by 1 John 4:19."*

147. *"I am a pillar in the temple of God. - Inspired by Revelation 3:12."*

148. *"I am a seeker of His wisdom and understanding. - Inspired by Proverbs 4:7."*

149. *"I am a delight in His eyes. - Inspired by Zephaniah 3:17."*

150. *"I am a masterpiece, created for His good works. - Inspired by Ephesians 2:10."*

Remember, these affirmations are your spiritual armor. Wear them daily, believe in them, and watch the transformation in your life. Your spiritual journey is uniquely yours. Embrace it, cherish it, and seek the Divine in every moment. Let's keep winning in our quest for deeper connections. God bless."

Acknowledgments

From the depth of my heart, thank you. I am overwhelmed with gratitude that you chose to journey with me through the pages of "*Talk That Talk*". My sincerest hope is that these affirmations echo in your heart and mind, inspiring you to bravely stride on your path to personal and professional success.

My family - my beautiful wife and our three amazing daughters - thank you for being my anchor and guiding light. Your unwavering love, support, and belief in me have been the bedrock upon which I've built my dreams.

I want to take a moment to remember my father, who is no longer with us in body but continues to live in our hearts. Dad, your wisdom, strength, and spirit were my first guiding lights. You paved the way, making my journey smoother, and for that, I am forever grateful.

To my extended family, friends, church family, and those who passed through my life for a season - collectively, you are my village. You've celebrated my victories, supported me through my struggles, and added immeasurable value to my life. This book is a testament to the impact you've had on my journey.

A special thank you to my hometown, Compton, for the tough lessons, the losses, and the gains. Thank you for fostering my growth and reminding me it's not where you start. It's where you're going. Compton, you've played a crucial role in molding me into the man I am today.

I am indebted to the mentors and leaders who have come before me. Their wisdom and teachings have illuminated my path. Figures like Les Brown, Tony Robbins, Eric Thomas, Jim Rohn, and Inky Johnson - your influence reverberates through the words of this book.

My deepest gratitude goes to God, my shepherd and confidant. Through every challenge and victory, Your divine guidance has been my compass, and for that, I am eternally grateful.

Finally, to you, my dear reader - thank you for your time, your open mind, and your willingness to embrace the journey of self-improvement and growth. This book was written with you in mind. My hope is that it ignites within you the courage to "talk that talk", to walk with purpose, conviction, and confidence.

Remember, you are more than your possessions. You are valued. You are loved. You are a child of God with boundless potential and purpose. Let's continue this journey together, growing, learning, and transforming into the best versions of ourselves.

With deepest gratitude,

Robert Lawson Jr.

Share the Blessings

In life's intricate tapestry, every thread, every story, and every victory matters. Your journey, with its highs and lows, moments of doubt, and bursts of revelation, is a testament to the enduring human spirit. And if this book has played even a small role in guiding, uplifting, or transforming your path, then it's a shared victory. A victory not just for you, but for every soul out there seeking direction, hope, and affirmation.

But here's the beautiful part: blessings, when shared, multiply. They ripple out, touching lives in ways we might never even fathom. So, if you've found solace, strength, or inspiration in these pages, I urge you to pass it on. Gift this book to a friend navigating a storm, a colleague facing a crossroad, or a loved one in need of a beacon. Your gesture might just be the lifeline they've been seeking.

Moreover, your feedback, your stories, and your experiences breathe life into this endeavor. Please leave a review, share your journey, or reach out to me directly. Every word you share becomes a beacon for someone else, guiding them through their darkest nights and into the dawn of new possibilities.

In this vast universe, our connections, our shared stories, and our collective victories are the threads that weave us together. By sharing, you're not just passing on a book; you're passing on hope, faith, and the promise of a brighter tomorrow. Let's keep winning together, and as always, God bless.

What's Next?

Congratulations on completing "*Talk That Talk: How the Right Words Turn Negative Thoughts into Positive Vibes*." You've taken a monumental step toward transforming your mindset and, by extension, your life. But remember, the journey doesn't end here; it's just the beginning.

Take the Next Step with My Exclusive App:

To continue this transformative journey, I invite you to join our exclusive community through "**The Way We Win**" app. This isn't just an extension of the book; it's a whole new level of engagement, inspiration, and empowerment.

What You'll Get:

Audio Experience: Listen to me personally read the stories from the book, along with additional commentary and insights that aren't in the print version.

Community Support: Connect with like-minded individuals who are also on their journey of self-improvement. Share your experiences, challenges, and triumphs.

Custom Content: Get access to exclusive videos, articles, and more that are only available to our app community.

Direct Access: Participate in live Q&A sessions and webinars and get first access to new content and offerings.

And Much More: Surprises await! We're constantly updating the app with new features to help you keep winning.

How to Access:

Simply scan the QR code below (or visit the following URL: **https://TheWayWeWin.com/**) to download the app and unlock a treasure trove of resources designed to elevate your mindset and enrich your life.

Scan me

As a special thank-you for reading this book, you'll get free access to the digital version of "*Talk That Talk*" within the app.

Your journey towards a life dominated by positive affir-mations and mindset shifts is a marathon, not a sprint. Equip yourself with the right tools and community to make the journey not just transformative but also enjoyable.

Let's keep winning in our own unique ways. You got this. God bless.

With Gratitude and Blessings,

Robert Lawson Jr.

www.ingramcontent.com/pod-product-compliance
Lightning Source LLC
Chambersburg PA
CBHW051421090426
42737CB00014B/2776